MARK —

YOUR DREAMS ... [
TRYING TO TELL YOU
SOMETHING!

Best Wishes.

JGFord

For my wife Debbie:
In a life full of nightmares,
she is my dream girl.

From the Private Patient Files
of Dr. Ford Freud

www.mascotbooks.com

Dr. Ford Freud: A Cure For Nightmares

For more information, please contact:
Mascot Books
620 Herndon Parkway, Suite 320
Herndon, VA 20170
info@mascotbooks.com

Library of Congress Control Number: 2018904181

CPSIA Code: PROPM0918A
ISBN-13: 978-1-68401-837-6

Printed in the United States

Dr. Ford Freud:
A *CURE* FOR
NIGHTMARES

J. A. Ford
Book One of the Fordian Trilogy

Contents

PREFACE TO BOOK ONE

By Dr. Ford Freud, B.A., B.S., M.A., PhD., M.D., C.P.A., B.M.F.

A child's brain is a squishy gray abomination, much like the gruel that my mother used to serve me each morning for breakfast. And just like my mother's semi-congealed breakfast cereal, the brain of a child is too spongy to work particularly well, or for that matter act as a satisfactory doorstop. As a practitioner of the behavioral arts, I endeavor to make sense out of the chaotic pediatric brain and the irrational thoughts and emotions that spring from it. Where childhood irrationality is often at its most bizarre is in dreams and nightmares.

Even for adults with fully-formed brains, these nocturnal expeditions into the vagaries of the subconscious mind can be disturbing or confusing. Young children usually lack the ability to understand that dreams are not real. Some children can become so consumed with an irrational fear of what occurs in their dreams that they become emotionally unstable. This is often when an expert such as myself is called in to teach the child that he is exhibiting emotions that are not based upon reality and are therefore unacceptable.

To the scholars, healthcare practitioners, students, and other members of the enlightened populace who have wisely chosen to read this book: I bestow upon you my warmest salutations and greetings! When I was approached by this fine publisher suggesting that I write a series of books about my most unusual and interesting cases in the field of psychology, I initially had to demur. I explained to the publisher that I simply could not devote the amount of time that would be required to compose such a collection of stories. I explained to the publisher that because of my obligations to the university, my grant-funded research, and my active private practice, there were simply not enough hours in the day to devote to a new undertaking. This had become even more true because I had recently been elected President of the Society of New and Original Thinkers (S.N.O.T.) When the publisher suggested that another author could "ghost write" the series of books, I was both intrigued and hesitant. I made it clear to the publisher that such an author would need to have the skills and acumen to fully appreciate my work and the practical ramifications that my research on the workings of the human brain has had on society as a whole.

After receiving such assurances from the publisher, I opened my patient files and personal notes to the ghost writer/author, Mr. J. A. Ford. Further, I spent many hours with the author, sharing with him the thought process, deductions and reasoning that I applied to each patient's case. It is my belief that the author appreciates how my work in this field will at some time be regaled as a renaissance in the field of human cognition and behavior. Mr. Ford also performed research on his own so that he could get a grasp of the immense impact of my work. Mr. Ford has advised me that he has conducted many interviews with pertinent witnesses in order to collect all of the applicable facts and circumstances surrounding the cases.

To assure the professionalism and academic integrity of this book, the publisher has demanded that Mr. Ford's *magnum opus* not be seen by me until the final stage of the book's publication. Confident in my professional accomplishments and having been assured of the author's utmost professionalism, I have graciously agreed to this arrangement. Here, then, is the first book that examines my casework in the field of human behavior, pathopsychology, and the shadowy world of the pediatric mind.

Yours sincerely,
Dr. Ford Freud

CHAPTER ONE

Dr. Freud's Lecture

Early May was usually not this hot and was almost *never* this humid. Despite the sweltering 95 degrees and palpable humidity, a long line of people stood outside of Arts & Sciences Hall, waiting to be allowed to enter. Most of the men wore business suits but had removed their jackets and draped them across their arms. Some of the women shaded their faces with their pocketbooks, and many waved their hands in front of their faces to fan themselves. When the doors opened, the crowd politely but quickly moved into the building. They were eager to get a good seat in the lecture hall and were also happy to get out of the sun. More than 150 undergraduates, graduate students, faculty, and guests packed the stuffy lecture hall.

The large classroom was built like a half-shell amphitheater. At the bottom of the amphitheater was the teacher's podium, which was flanked on either side by long blackboards. For those who were only able to get seats in the back rows, the podium looked very small. Unfortunately, very few of the lecture halls at the university were equipped with air conditioning. The heat and humidity joined together that day to make the lecture hall uncomfortably hot and sticky. A handful of metal fans had been brought into the classroom, but they really provided no relief at all. Many of the students who brought binders or pads for note-taking were using them as fans. The students who sat through hours of lectures had become accustomed to the lecture hall's smell on hot and stagnant days like this. The thick air smelled like sweat, old wood, and decades of accumulated chalk dust. The unfortunates in the back row were even more uncomfortable than those who had secured seats closer to the bottom. They could feel the temperature rise as they walked up the steep steps towards the back of the room. Each step meant a little more heat and humidity that would have to be endured.

Despite the uncomfortable venue, even the people in the back row were very pleased to be in attendance. They were going to be treated to a lecture from a visiting professor whose reputation as a great scholar and a skillful medical clinician was unequalled.

Mr. and Mrs. Bracken got in line an hour before the lecture's start time, so they could be assured seats in the front of the classroom, as close as possible to the guest speaker. They ended up with excellent seats in the second row, directly in front of the podium. Mrs. Bracken's face flushed and the leg that she crossed over the other was a pendulum that swung nervously up and down.

"Do you think he will?" she asked her husband for the umpteenth time that afternoon.

"I hope so, Becky," he replied, gently patting her hand. With much effort, he smiled a little and added, "Yes, I think he will." Sweat was running down his torso and he could the feel the stream stop when it reached the pistol that was tucked into the waistband of his pants. He nervously patted the front of his shirt, which was concealing the weapon. As uncomfortable as the bulky pistol was, he felt better knowing that he had it. Although he could have concealed the pistol in another manner, he felt more confident when he could actually feel the metal weapon touching his skin.

She momentarily returned her husband's kind smile but it vanished almost immediately. Stress and concern had ravaged her young face; the dark bags under her eyes showed the vestiges of her burdens.

When the chancellor of the university and the guest lecturer arrived in the classroom, the room burst into applause. The chancellor was taken aback by the applause, as he was not accustomed to such an enthusiastic ovation. The guest lecturer, however, anticipated and expected such a reception when he walked into a room. The chancellor straightened his tie and approached the podium to address the audience. The crowd stopped clapping and became silent when the chancellor raised his hand.

"Ladies and gentlemen, one of the great honors that is bestowed upon the university chancellor is the opportunity to introduce scholars who are at the cutting edge of their profession. All of you have come here today because you obviously understand the importance of the work that has been done by today's honored and esteemed guest lecturer. It is my belief that as we approach the bicentennial of these United States of America, we should take time to truly appreciate the progress that has been achieved in all of the arts and sciences during this country's brief existence. In order to achieve this degree of appreciation, we need to take the opportunity to study and share in the experiences of those who will be our leaders as we begin the third century of this great country."

The audience applauded politely, and the chancellor took this opportunity to wipe the sweat off of his upper lip with his monogrammed handkerchief. "How should I introduce today's esteemed guest lecturer? Statesman? Scholar? Professor? Scientist? Clinical psychologist? How about all of the above?" The audience laughed politely. "Maybe it's best if I just introduce the man and let you decide which accolades should be used to describe him. This university is honored to welcome Dr. Ford Freud."

The audience's applause for the professor was loud and enthusiastic. Mrs. Bracken clapped heartily, glancing at her husband with hopeful eyes. The elderly Dr. Freud shook the chancellor's hand and stepped up to the podium. Earlier that afternoon, the chancellor asked the professor if he wanted to use a microphone but the doctor's reply was that he would consider it a dishonor to use such a device. He explained that the gathered were entitled to hear his voice without any type of "electrical enhancement." Although he was wearing a heavy camel hair sport coat and a dress shirt with a collar that was a bit tight, there was initially no sign of perspiration on the professor's face. A billowy gray beard covered up the sweat that had formed on his cheeks and chin.

When the audience became silent, Dr. Freud cleared his throat and addressed them with his booming, authoritative voice. "We have come to an important time in the development of the human race," he announced to his rapt audience. "Over the past one hundred years, we have studied and solved most of the mysteries of the human brain. The human brain is no longer a scary monster that should be feared. We have discovered all of the brain's secrets and consequently scientists are no longer blindly stumbling through the realm of human behavior.

"Consider what we currently know of the brain at sleep. For centuries, the popular belief was that dreams were a dimension where nefarious spirits and demons assaulted our brains and tried to take over our souls. At the turn of the nineteenth century, many learned scholars hypothesized that our dreams were a way for us to deal with internal conflicts. We were told that dreams were a mechanism by which we addressed thorny personal issues. The popular belief at that time was that if you dreamt about collecting seashells, it was because of the trauma you endured when you were potty trained." Some of the audience chuckled at the absurdity of this notion. "There was a Dr. Freud who wrote an entire book about the interpretation of dreams but I can assure you he is not in my lineage!" Again, the attendees laughed at the quip. "No, I am the Dr. Freud who believes only in facts and substance. Dreams definitely don't delve deeply into our subconscious mind. Through research conducted by myself, we now realize that our dreams are nothing more than harmless vignettes put on by our brains for our amusement. Sometimes the movies produced by our brains are funny, amorous, bizarre or frightening, just like the selection of movies showing at the cinema. Some are poorly structured, while others are very detailed and logical. Once we realized that these were nothing more than amusements created by our brains while they lie dormant during our sleep, we no longer looked for deep-seated reasons for our dreams. We now just accept them for what they are: harmless and meaningless one act plays produced by our brain.

"What we now must do is focus on the implementation and practice of what we have learned. Our universities are the means to train the next generation of psychologists who will take the knowledge that we have collected and apply it with vigor to their patients and to their communities." Once again there was enthusiastic applause from the audience. "We have overcome polio. We have overcome two world wars. We even overcame the craziness of the late 1960's." Laughter filled the hall and the professor smiled. "Now that we have overcome these challenges, we need to use our knowledge of human behavior to keep the masses from regressing into absurd and superstitious beliefs. As I have conducted the important research in the field of pediatric psychology, I have had to convince people that old wives' tales and *rules of thumb* should be abandoned. Sometimes that has been a very difficult task. We, as learned scholars, need to explain to the populace that science has shown us all of the truths of the universe. All we have to do is to have the courage to accept and disseminate that knowledge."

For 90 minutes, the professor provided the rapt audience with an abbreviated summary of the major milestones that had been established in the areas of clinical and pediatric psychology during the 63 years that Dr. Freud had been alive. Dr. Freud paid no attention to the sweat dripping into his eyes and saturating his mustache and beard. The professor was energetic throughout his lecture and urged all in attendance to reach for the highest goals in their field of study. He further encouraged the students to take the theoretical concepts they were taught at the university and make them practical so that they could impact others and improve their lives.

As the applause subsided and Dr. Freud was about to step away from the podium, the chancellor approached him, carrying something large that had been covered with black velvet. "Before you finish, Dr. Freud, the faculty and administration are proud to bestow upon you our university's greatest academic honor." The crowd erupted in cheers and applause. The chancellor had to wait a few moments for it to fade before continuing with the presentation. "As you may already know, our proud university is the home of the Twin Gold Owls." A few of the undergraduate students in the audience stood up and chanted in unison, "Go Gold Owl One! Go Gold Owl Two! Gold Owls Hoot Hoot Hoot!"

More applause erupted and Dr. Freud smiled, appreciative of the assembled crowd's enthusiasm. "With all of these owls around, I guess it's a good thing I did not bring one of my lab rats with me today!" Dr. Freud joked, causing the crowd to laugh and clap appreciatively. "Owls and rats don't typically mix well in polite company!"

The chancellor chuckled and then continued his presentation. "As a result, we are proud to present to you, Dr. Freud, membership into the Sacred Order of the Golden Twin Hooters!" With a flourish, the chancellor whipped off the black velvet. Perched on a thick wooden base were two life-sized metal owls that had been painted in glimmering gold flake paint. The two owls were proud and defiant, with their chests proudly puffed out. Many men in the audience found the area where the wings of the two owls touched each other oddly appealing to the eye. The crowd applauded as the chancellor handed the award to Dr. Freud.

"I am honored to accept this prestigious award," Dr. Freud announced with a beaming face. "If anyone asks me about my trip to this university, I shall proudly display this pair," he said, holding up the award. "Although, if I am ever invited back to this university, I'll ask to return when it's a little cooler!" Once again, the crowd laughed and applauded.

After the lecture and award ceremony were completed, the professor shook many hands. He gladly autographed copies of his books that audience members held out to him. The chancellor appointed himself as a *de facto* concert manager and roadie for Dr. Freud. His primary goal was to make Dr. Freud's visit to the university as organized and pleasant as possible. The first person in line to meet Dr. Freud was a graduate student from the clinical psychology program who politely asked the doctor to sign a copy of Freud's seminal treatise *"What If The Patients Are Fine And We Are All Insane?"* The chancellor smiled as the graduate student thanked Dr. Freud and shook his hand.

"Just one pump of the hand: nothing crazy. Professional. Good," the chancellor thought.

As soon as the lady and her husband hurriedly stepped towards Dr. Freud, the chancellor could tell there was going to be trouble. The woman's eyes were wild, as if she was on some type of stimulant. Her husband was holding lovingly onto her arm in order to try to control her but he was failing miserably. The chancellor's first thought was that an assault or assassination of the famous Dr. Freud while at the university would be a public relations nightmare. Before the chancellor could step in and intervene, the woman clamped onto a sleeve of Dr. Freud's sport coat and dropped to her knees.

"Please! Dr. Freud, we need you!" she pleaded with tears in her eyes. "Our son! Our son!" She said some other things after that but she was so hysterical the chancellor couldn't understand what she was saying.

The chancellor tried to pull the woman to her feet, but her legs were wet noodles. "Madam, I'm going to have to ask you to leave the premises. This isn't the time nor the place for this kind of spectacle," chided the chancellor.

Dr. Freud put his hand on the chancellor's shoulder and said, "Please, let me talk to her. She's obviously in need of my expert assistance."

When the woman heard the renowned doctor's kind words, she smiled and said, "Thank you, doctor, thank you."

"Madam, I am contractually obligated to greet some students and faculty," Dr. Freud said kindly. "If you would be willing to patiently wait for me, I promise to grant you an audience so that we can talk about what has upset you. Would that be acceptable, kind lady?"

She nodded her head repeatedly and told him again how thankful she was. The doctor smiled, turned to the chancellor, and asked, "Do you have someone who could get her a cool drink so that she can get refreshed before we discuss her situation?"

The chancellor was stupefied at how quickly and effectively Dr. Freud had diffused the emotionally volatile situation. Once he'd ushered the woman and her husband to a quiet classroom next to the lecture hall, the chancellor thought to himself, "Of course he handled the situation perfectly: he's a behavioral science genius!"

It took the doctor more than hour to shake all the hands he needed to shake and pose for photographs. As soon as he completed these duties, Dr. Freud asked the chancellor where the woman had been taken. Without hesitation, the doctor went to the classroom and saw that her husband was stroking her hand, attempting to keep her calm.

"I apologize for taking so long," Dr. Freud said. "I anticipated that I would be able to tend to your problem a little sooner but the crowd couldn't get enough of me. Alas, that is my plight."

"We're just happy that you could make time for us," the man said. "We're at wit's end, as you probably already guessed. We didn't know if you'd even talk to normal people, you know, like us."

Dr. Freud took a seat at one of the desks and held the woman's hands gently in his own. "My oath as a psychologist and a physician calls upon me to help those in need to the very best of my abilities. I may or may not be able to help you. It is my solemn duty, however, to either assist you myself or to put you in the hands of a professional who can help you in your hour of need. To begin with, tell me who I have the honor of speaking with tonight."

"My name's David Bracken and this is my wife Becky. We're here because we're scared to death about our son Jeremy."

"Jeremy is having horrible problems with crazy dreams and nightmares. He has them every night. They're taking away my little boy!" Mrs. Bracken said, her upper lip quivering a little.

"It's true what my wife says. Lots of nights we hear him screaming and we have to calm him down. He doesn't tell us very much about the dreams. He says he can't remember them but they must be really bad to make him scream like that."

When Dr. Freud was in thought, he often stroked his mustache and beard with his right hand. As he squeezed his upper lip with his thumb and index finger, the doctor asked, "How long has this been going on?"

"A little more than six months," Mr. Bracken replied. "Some nights it's worse than other times but it's been pretty consistent." There was a pause as Dr. Freud began to consider potential diagnoses. To fill the awkward silence, Mr. Bracken added, "You've no idea what it's like to have your son scream so loud that it jerks you out of a sound sleep."

"Quite so. Is there any family history of sleep disturbances or night terrors?" the doctor asked.

"Night terrors? Is that the same as a nightmare?" Mrs. Bracken asked.

"There are textbook differences between nightmares and night terrors but they can be difficult to differentiate even in a clinical setting."

Mr. Bracken looked at his wife and when she shook her head, he said to the doctor, "Not that we know of."

"We would need to investigate how the patient responds to being awakened, whether he has feelings of terror during multiple sleep cycles and whether there are concurrent physiologic manifestations," Dr. Freud explained in a matter-of-fact tone.

The Brackens didn't understand most of what the doctor said and they looked at the doctor with wide, uncomprehending eyes. Dr. Freud realized that he'd mistakenly spoken to them as if they were fellow professors. "I apologize, that must have sounded like a whole lot of nonsense to untrained people like you. In plainer words, I would need to talk to the patient and examine him before reaching any definitive and final conclusions."

"Would you...even consider..." Mrs. Bracken stammered.

"Yes, I'd be happy to talk to the patient. I could suggest that a different doctor see the patient, but there is not going to be anybody who knows about this area as much as I do, so I feel obligated to step in. I can change my return flight arrangements and see the patient tomorrow morning here at the university, if that is acceptable with you."

Launching herself at the doctor, Mrs. Bracken kissed his cheek and thanked him over and over again.

CHAPTER TWO

All Hallows' Eve

Most of us have forgotten what it was to think like an eight-year-old child. Case in point: a child's failure to grasp the idea you can actually have *too much* of a good thing. Overindulgence is a concept that is hard for a kid to understand. If one ride on a Ferris wheel is good and a second ride is fantastic, it's reasonable in the child's mind to conclude that twenty rides would be awesome beyond belief. Adults can try to explain to the child that the fun will likely go away after about the fifth ride, and he will probably puke-up his corndog and cotton candy after the fifteenth, but it would probably be a waste of time. Most kids don't understand the well-accepted rule of thumb that too much of a good thing is bad. Once they have polished off a tasty piece of chocolate cake with sugary whipped frosting, there's no reason they can think of as to why they shouldn't have another piece. Or a third piece. Or a sixth.

According to a publication written by renowned pediatric psychologist Dr. Ford Freud, when parents tell a child he can only have *one* piece of cake, there is a disconnect in the child's developing brain. "Why would my parents, who love me, want to keep me from eating one of the most wonderful things I've ever tasted?" To the child, the oft-used explanation that doing so would spoil your supper is meaningless. So what if you spoiled your supper? Something that tasted this good had to be better than anything else mom could cook for supper.

On the other hand, the concept of *serendipity* is something that kids sometimes understand better than adults. Dr. Freud has explained that in the logical and regimented adult world, everything must have a cause and effect. If something bad happens, then there must have been an identifiable cause. A kid's world, however, is full of daily events wherein something "just happens." Food appears in the refrigerator. The furnace warms up and the air conditioner magically cools. It just happens. Serendipity.

When Jeremy Bracken was eight years old, overindulgence and serendipity collided into each other, creating an ordeal that was much larger than the mere sum of its parts. It was during this time that Jeremy's life changed in a very profound way.

October 31, 1975, was going to be Jeremy's fourth trick-or-treat experience in his short life. As he figured, all of his previous Halloween experiences were merely dress rehearsals leading up to the carefully orchestrated candy onslaught he planned for 1975. Jeremy remembered very little about the brisk night in 1972 when he trick-or-treated for the very first time. There was a snapshot in the photo album of five-year-old Jeremy draped in an ill-fitting homemade costume and holding a brown paper grocery bag. His mom had dressed him in one of his father's old business suits. As an added touch, she smeared a little Vaseline on his chin and sprinkled it with coffee grounds to make it look like Jeremy had whisker stubble. As best as he could remember, his parents had only taken him to a handful houses that night. When he was six, he was allowed to walk up to the door on his own but his father was trailing him. His father told him that the only reason he was tagging along was to make sure that none of the older kids stole his candy along the way.

Halloween in 1974 was special because Jeremy was finally old enough to go out with his friends without being shadowed by a lurking parent. Before he left the house, his mother gave him a long list of things to avoid such as barking dogs, men in cars, and older kids who were vandalizing property. It was an amazing journey that Jeremy talked about all the way to Christmas. Caving into relentless lobbying by Jeremy, his mother bought the good kind of costume made by the Ben Cooper Company. It was sold in a colorful, flimsy paperboard box with the mask staring blankly from behind a sheet of cellophane. Inside was a onesie that made the identity of the costume obvious to all who saw it. Spider-Man had his insignia emblazoned on the chest, and the cowboy had chaps and a gun belt printed on the costume. Most of the kids had to stretch the costume over their clothes because their mothers wanted them to stay warm while they were running around in the crisp October air. Jeremy and his pals ran from house to house, eagerly collecting candy in their neighborhood. It was a great adventure! Could life be any better than gallivanting around the neighborhood with your buddies and collecting loads of free candy? Jeremy didn't think so. They started their trek at 6:30 and did not return to their homes until 8:00. While they were walking back home, Jeremy saw that there were still a few houses that had yet to turn their porch lights off. If a couple of his friends had not gotten tired, Jeremy could have put in at least another half hour.

When he got home, his parents were surprised to see the impressive size of his haul. The brown paper grocery bag that he carried was nearly half full with treats! Almost immediately, the bag of candy was whisked away and placed in the cabinet above the refrigerator by his mother. His parents explained that the bag of candy was only open for business at certain times of the day. Over the following weeks, the candy was rationed out by his parents.

When Halloween 1975 was only a week away, Jeremy called together a summit of his closest friends to discuss the details of their upcoming onslaught of the neighborhood's candy supply. All of the boys at the meeting were eight years old, except for Rob, who had already turned nine. The boys got together at the baseball diamond and talked about the pressing issue of parental interference with their Halloween candy. All of the members of this brain trust shared with the group that they had endured similar restrictions on the consumption of their candy. The flow of sugary goodness was so slow that some kids reported that they were still drawing from their bag of candy after Thanksgiving. Jeremy encouraged the group to suggest ways to avoid this parental restriction on the flow of candy. As was typical, the kids who had older siblings had the most information to share with the group. They knew what schemes their older brothers and sisters had tried and what pitfalls could occur. The advisability of hiding a stash of candy in your bedroom closet was debated. Tales of dogs, cats, siblings and even a mouse getting into the hidden stashes were shared. Stories of hiding candy outside always ended poorly. Even when cleverly hidden in heavily fortified tree forts, the stash of candy was inevitably ravaged by rain, snow, squirrels, or thieves. Despite the significant collection of Halloween experts that had been assembled, the summit couldn't come up with a fool-proof solution. Once all meaningful discussions had been exhausted, the members of the summit divided up and played cowboys and Indians.

Like a soldier preparing for battle, Jeremy laid out his gear on his bed the night before Halloween. After finding grocery bags too fragile, he told his mother than he needed an old pillowcase to carry his loot. He had grown a fair amount in the past year, so his Batman costume was too small. In order to get one more year out of the costume, his mother used scissors to slice darts in the legs and down the middle of the back of the onesie. Even with these alterations, it barely fit over the top of Jeremy's jeans and sweatshirt. The sleeves only came down to just below his elbows. Luckily, it was unseasonably warm that year in the Midwest, so Jeremy didn't have to try to pull the costume over a bulky winter coat. The brittle, gray rubber band on his mask had broken shortly into last year's mission. Dad had threaded an old shoestring through holes on each side of the mask. Jeremy didn't own sneakers, but he had an old pair of shoes that were well-worn and good for running. Jeremy carefully chose which friends would accompany him. His plan was to cover a large area in a short amount of time, so any of his buddies who weren't up for an aggressive attack on the neighborhood's candy wouldn't be invited to join the elite strike force.

The night before Halloween, Jeremy laid in bed and stared at the dark bedroom ceiling. Jeremy and three friends made a pact to aggressively scour the area and liberate as much candy as possible the following evening. They discussed where the greatest density of houses was located and how they could cover the greatest amount of territory. As he ran through their basic battle plans in his head, it was no wonder that Jeremy found it difficult to fall asleep. Eventually he nodded off with thoughts of sweet Halloween candies on his mind and a smile on his face.

As long as he could remember, Jeremy had colorful and detailed dreams. That night, he dreamt that he was riding a toboggan down a hill covered with slick chocolate frosting. When the sled got to the bottom of the hill, Jeremy was catapulted forward, landing in a large mound of Tootsie Rolls. Swimming out of the candy, he smelled the faint, wonderful scent of milk chocolate. He picked up one of the Tootsie Rolls and tried to unwrap it, but it was sealed tight and wouldn't open. Jeremy couldn't remember what happened next in his dream.

Despite not sleeping very well the night before, the four boys were full of energy and they covered a lot of ground on Halloween night. Batman, Spiderman, the Lone Ranger and a hobo scurried as a group from house to house. Houses with no lights on were ignored, as the group had no time for pranks or retribution against these party poopers. After a treat was dropped into their bags, they didn't take time to analyze the type or size of the candy, as this would just slow them down. Besides, there'd be plenty of time to do that analysis on November 1st. The Four Horsemen of the Candy Apocalypse raced through multiple neighborhoods, autumn's brittle leaves crunching under their shoes. For the first hour, they were able to maintain a very fast pace, running and laughing as they went from house to house. Contrary to his mother's instructions, Jeremy and his friends did *not* use the sidewalks and instead across yards to cover more ground.

They slowed down a little during the second hour but not much. By the end of the second hour, a few houses had turned off their lights, and this pumped new energy and a sense of urgency into the group of costumed characters. By 8:45, most of the houses had closed up shop, so the group started walking towards home. As they did so, they recounted the night's success with excited voices, sometimes leering into their bags and running their hands through the treasures they had amassed. It was 9:00 by the time they were back in their own neighborhood. Since he knew that his bag of candy would be confiscated as soon as he got home, Jeremy suggested to his friends that they take a few minutes before returning home to gorge themselves on candy.

Sitting on a curb under a streetlight, they had a contest to see how much candy each of them could stuff into their mouths at once. Jeremy stuffed some little candy bars, a few bites of a popcorn ball, and a string of licorice into his mouth. This odd combination of sugary goodness tasted wonderful! The boys' hands couldn't unwrap the treats fast enough. As soon as they freed the candy from its wrapper, it was popped into the mouth. There were times that they had the tastes of multiple kinds of candy in their mouths all at the same time. Jeremy figured that he was making his *own* kind of Halloween treat in his mouth. Had anyone ever taken chocolate, peanut brittle, and licorice and ground it up into a gravy? Was anyone willing to add a few bites of a sweet popcorn ball to this concoction? No matter what combination of goodies he tried, Jeremy thought that the outcome was delicious. Jeremy and his friends concluded that this was apparently what the adults didn't want them to experience and why they controlled the flow of candy. They didn't want the kids creating unique and crazy combinations of goodness. It was alright for you to have all of the ingredients of the mish-mash, but if you dared to mix them altogether, you were venturing into forbidden territory.

When he walked up the porch steps of his house, Jeremy's stomach was churning and he wasn't feeling very well. Great explorers and trailblazers usually paid a price for their expeditions into uncharted territory, and Jeremy was no different. He felt like the area below his belly button was being inflated with an air pump. The pain came in waves. At times he felt like his innards were being twisted. As he anticipated, the bag of candy was sequestered in the cupboard above the refrigerator by his mom shortly after he walked through the front door. Jeremy didn't make a fuss because he had no interest in candy at that point. When his mother tucked him in, she noticed that he was wincing.

"How much candy did you eat while you were out there?" she asked in an accusatory tone.

"Just a little," Jeremy sheepishly replied.

"Yeah, I bet," she said, slowly shaking her head. She brought a wastepaper basket into Jeremy's bedroom and put it by the bed. "Just in case you need it," she said, pointing at it. "Love you, honey," she added as she left his room.

It was a rough night. His belly pain didn't subside and it was bad enough to keep him up most of the night. At one point, he stared at the wastepaper basket that was illuminated by the moonlight coming through his bedroom window. He considered sticking his finger down his throat, in hopes that a long course of vomiting would give him some relief. Throwing up, he thought, might reduce the pressure that was building up in his stomach. At one point he got his hand all the way to his lips before pulling it back. Jeremy decided to just ride the storm out. It ended up being a very long and tortuous storm.

CHAPTER THREE
The Man in the Dark Suit

Even though his stomach still hurt the next morning, Jeremy was initially anxious to go to school so that he could regale everyone with the accomplishments of his group. It was clear to his mother, however, that Jeremy needed to stay home. The rough night had left Jeremy sleepy and lethargic. In addition to his pain, Jeremy had developed a significant amount of nausea, and he refused to eat or drink anything at breakfast. He vomited a little bit shortly before noon. This provided some momentary reduction of the pressure he felt building in his stomach. The waves of pain quickly returned, however, and continued throughout the rest of the day.

When his father came home from work, he was surprised to see that Jeremy was still nauseous and having significant abdominal pain. By suppertime, his parents became increasingly concerned that this was something more than just an overindulgence of Halloween candy and decided to take Jeremy to the hospital. In the emergency room, Jeremy endured multiple examinations of his abdomen. Doctors and nurses pressed on his stomach and poked their fingers up into his groin. Sometimes the pain was bad enough that Jeremy felt a little short of breath. After an x-ray was taken, a doctor reported that Jeremy had what was called a *small bowel obstruction.*

"If it's just a *small* obstruction, why does it hurt so much?" Jeremy asked his mother in a forlorn voice.

"I don't know, honey," she soothed as she stroked his hair.

"Sometimes it just happens like that."

The emergency room doctor patted Jeremy on the shoulder and said, "We'll have you stay here in the hospital tonight, big guy. We'll get you fixed up in no time."

Jeremy was moved to a gurney and wheeled to another part of the hospital. As they walked alongside the gurney, his parents talked to Jeremy continuously, trying to keep their son's mind from the daunting realization that he'd be spending the night alone in the hospital.

"Lots of people go to the hospital," his mother said cheerfully.

"Sure. Even Batman needs to go to the hospital sometimes," his father reassured.

"You'll be just fine, honey," his mother soothed with a concerned smile on her face.

As he was about to push Jeremy into his hospital room, the orderly said, "Your roommate's name is Tommy. He's sleeping. Tommy's having surgery tomorrow, so we need to be quiet so he can sleep."

He was pushed into the room and past a boy who was sleeping soundly. Jeremy scooted off the gurney and onto his hospital bed. Once Jeremy was sitting up in his bed, the orderly pulled a curtain so that the room was divided and Jeremy could no longer see Tommy. The emergency room doctor had given Jeremy a shot in his butt right before he got on the gurney. By the time he got to his room, his pain was not as intense. The waves of cramping and nausea, however, continued to wash over Jeremy. It still felt like he had really bad gas but he never farted, so the pressure in his belly just got progressively worse.

A nurse who was as wide as she was tall pulled back the curtain and waddled into the room carrying a small silver tray. "According to the paperwork, Master Jeremy has an order for an NG tube. Mmmhm. And just take a guess at who gets to do the honors!"

"A what?" Jeremy asked, snapping his head and glaring at his mother. "What's an *enjee*?" He had heard of an *engine* and an *injun* but he had never heard anyone talk about an *enjee*. He didn't like the sound of it and all his muscles tensed.

His father sensed the fear in his son's voice and quickly assured him, "It's something to make you get better."

Jeremy was old enough to know that things that were designed *to make you feel better* either tasted horrible or hurt like heck. He grabbed his mother's arm with one hand and his dad's with the other. He didn't say anything but his eyes were frantically darting from one parent to the other. Jeremy silently contemplated, "How far away could I get if I jumped out of the bed and ran out of here as fast as I can?"

"It would be best if mom and dad left the room while I get this done," the nurse said. When his mother did not immediately leave, the nurse added, "Go on, it'll just take me a minute or two. I've done lots of these." The nurse laid the tray on the nightstand and gestured towards the door.

After a bit of hesitation, his parents obeyed the order of the lady in the starched white dress and left the room.

"Let's get this done lickety split, Master Jeremy," the nurse said, turning her back to him as she leaned forward over the tray. Jeremy couldn't see what she was doing but he heard the sound of ripping of paper, as if she was opening a birthday present. After stuffing something into the large pocket located over her left thigh, she turned back around and looked at Jeremy with an insincere smile on her face. It was such an effort for her to smile that the end result was her facial expression looked sinister. She had a Q-tip as long as a pencil in her hand and there was a wad of greasy stuff perched on the cotton tip. For a moment, Jeremy relaxed just a little because he'd never had any kind of bad experience with a Q-tip. They were harmless. Right?

In one swift motion, the nurse put her left hand on Jeremy's forehead and pushed the unusually long Q-tip into his nostril. The invasion of his nose surprised Jeremy. It felt unpleasant to have the gooey Q-tip inside his nose but thankfully it didn't hurt. She pulled the Q-tip out of his nose and reached into her pocket. The nurse withdrew a long brown rubbery tube from her pocket and Jeremy's eyes got big. She started pushing the tube into his nose before Jeremy had time to object. When he squirmed, her left hand pressed even harder down on his forehead. Jeremy felt the brown snake go up into his nasal cavity and then begin sliding down the back of this throat. As he breathed through his mouth, he thought he could taste the rubber tube. It tasted the way a new Pink Pearl eraser smelled.

As she continued to push the tube down into Jeremy's stomach, her face was very close to his. He felt frozen and was left to simply gaze at the ugly black wart that was above her upper lip. He wasn't sure how long she pushed on the rubber tube but it seemed like an awfully long time. Eventually she stood back and said, "That wasn't so bad, was it?"

Jeremy had a long piece of rubber tubing dangling out of his nose and even more of it inside his body. What he wanted to yell was, "Are you crazy? That was horrible!" Jeremy didn't say anything and just nodded his head a little, tears welling up in his eyes. He wasn't sure if he still had the ability to speak since he now had a long brown tube snaking through his nose, down the back of his throat and presumably down into his guts. Jeremy also thought it would be unwise to rebuke the lady who had the ability to deftly thread a rubber hose into his body.

The nurse hooked up the portion of the hose that was hanging out of his nose to a glass container the size of a milk bottle. Once that was connected, his parents were permitted to return to the room.

His dad tried to sound upbeat and said, "That should fix you up, sport!"

His mom got light-headed when she saw the blackish fluid slowly dribbling into the bottle from the rubber tube. The nurse talked to his parents about something called *decompression of the bowel,* but Jeremy couldn't understand the particulars of the conversation. As the adults were talking, he ran his tongue across the roof of his mouth and back towards his tonsils. He gently probed the back of his throat with his tongue but he couldn't reach the rubber tubing. It seemed as though he ought to have been able to touch the tube with the tip of his tongue but he wasn't able to do so. He slowly slid his hand up towards the tubing but the nurse saw him and she slapped his hand, ordering him to leave it alone. Once the nurse (from that point he thought of her as "Nasty Nurse") left the room, he talked to his parents about the uncomfortable and nasty tasting tube, begging them to pull it out. He scrunched up his nose and tried to expel the tube from his body by gagging.

"Don't fight it, honey," his mother said. "Let it help you get better." She tried to look confident and loving, but Jeremy could see that she was scared.

His parents stayed at his bedside until the last possible moment, but all visitors were required to leave the hospital at 9:00. Nasty Nurse came back to the room to usher them out. Sleeping away from his parents was something that Jeremy had done before at summer camp and when he stayed overnight with his grandparents. He wasn't a little boy anymore and the prospect of staying overnight in the hospital shouldn't have scared him. But it did.

His father took Jeremy's hands in his own and looked intently at Jeremy. "I need you to be my brave little man. Do you think you can do that, son?"

Jeremy promised his dad that he'd be brave but deep down

he was still scared. After the adults left, Jeremy sat quietly in his bed, listening to the sounds of the hospital. There always seemed to be someone talking or walking in the hallway outside of his and Tommy's room. He momentarily turned on the television but there was nothing interesting on any of the three channels, so he turned it off. Jeremy closed his eyes and tried to relax. He thought about how much fun he and his friends had on Halloween. Jeremy smiled when he thought of the big bag of candy waiting for him at home. Nasty Nurse suddenly whipped back the curtain and Jeremy nearly jumped out of his hospital smock.

"You doin' alright, Master Jeremy?" she asked in a sharp voice. Jeremy assured her that he was fine, and although he would never have admitted it to her, Jeremy was actually relieved to see her familiar, albeit sour face.

He closed his eyes again and tried to relax. Eventually he fell asleep. Before the sun had risen, Jeremy suddenly jerked out of a deep sleep. He was disoriented and momentarily panicked when he realized he wasn't in his bedroom. Somewhere in the back of his mind, he recalled being told to push a red button if he needed help. When he noticed that there was a small red button on the bed rail, he started pushing it frantically. It was then that he noticed that there was something that was in his nose which felt as though it was snaking down the back of his throat. Still groggy and tired, Jeremy put his hand up to his nose and was surprised to feel a piece of rubber tubing. He pulled a little on the tube but did so tentatively, as he was unsure what it was connected to. It was when he was gently tugging on the tube that Nasty Nurse pulled back the curtain.

"Stop that! Let it go!" she shouted, her bellowing voice reverberating in the quiet hospital room. She roughly slapped his hand away from the tube. "Now you done it, young man!"

She strapped his hands to the bed rails quickly and by the time she'd done so, Jeremy's memory had mostly returned. He remembered that he was in the hospital because of a small problem with his bowel.

"Try to get out of that!" she said triumphantly as she waddled out of the room.

Jeremy got no more sleep that night. It wasn't the foul tasting rubber hose running down the back of his throat that kept him awake. After having the tube in his stomach for several hours, he finally got used to the sensation that there was something running down the back of his throat. What kept him awake was the fact that his wrists were tethered to the bedrails. He didn't realize how much shifting and repositioning it took to get comfortable until the tethers prevented him from doing so. Just about the time he got comfortable and started to doze off, one of his muscles would demand to be shifted into a different position. When Jeremy couldn't comply with this demand, the muscle started to ache.

Shortly before his folks arrived the next morning, a new nurse with a kind smile and a soothing voice visited Jeremy. She had beautiful brown eyes, the color of milk chocolate.

"If I take off these restraints, can I trust you to leave the NG tube alone?" the kind, friendly nurse asked.

After he eagerly nodded his head, Nice Nurse untied his wrists. As she removed his bondage, Jeremy instantly fell in love as he stared into her dark brown eyes.

Jeremy remained in bed all day. When visiting hours started at 9:00 that morning both of his parents were at his side and they did not leave until they were forced to do so at 9:00 that night. Since he didn't get very much sleep the previous night, he occasionally nodded-off while his parents were chatting. He was ordered not to get out of bed, so he had to pee into a plastic container that had a long neck on it. Jeremy thought it was lucky that he did not need to poo, as he had been told he would have to use a different device for that act, and it sounded like an unpleasant exercise. By late afternoon, his stomach was feeling a little better and he wasn't having as many gas pains. Since he wasn't permitted to have anything to eat, Jeremy wondered if some of the discomfort he was experiencing was simply due to the fact that he was hungry. Nice Nurse told Jeremy and his parents that once the pain in his belly stopped, the tube that went through his nose and into his stomach would likely be removed. She not only looked like an angel, she gave heavenly good news. Later that afternoon, everyone became even more upbeat when Jeremy reported that most of his pain had gone away. Because he was doing so well, Jeremy's parents reported that the tube might be removed by the doctor the next morning.

Nasty Nurse showed her sour face once again later that night. As she did the night before, she had the duty to shoo his parents out of the room at 9:00. Before they left, Nasty Nurse explained that because of the risk that he would pull the *enjee* tube out while he slept, they needed to strap Jeremy's wrists to the metal bed rails. Mom tied his wrists to the bed, saying that it was for his own protection. She kissed both of his hands and then his cheek before she and his father left. After checking that the restraints were adequately tied, Nasty Nurse turned off the light and pulled the curtain.

Some of the light from the hallway fell upon the flimsy curtain that separated the room, giving it an ambient glow. The thin curtain acted as a kind of nightlight. Jeremy heard Tommy snoring on the other side of the curtain. Some kind of machine was hooked up to his roommate and it broadcasted an annoying *beep*. Jeremy wondered if the stupid machine was designed to make sure he didn't go to sleep. *Beep. Beep.* If that was the machine's purpose, it was doing a good job, Jeremy thought. *Beep.*

Lying quietly in the dark hospital room, Jeremy heard his stomach making loud roaring noises. *Beep.* It was the same stomach sound that sometimes interrupted a quiet classroom when lunch time was approaching. *Beep.* Hungry. He was so hungry. A wonderful piece of chocolate, maybe a Three Musketeers, would taste really good right now. *Beep.* Or a big bowl of Kraft macaroni and cheese. Mmmm. Chocolate ice cream. *Beep.* Even though he was very tired, Jeremy thought that his grumbling stomach and that stupid beeping machine were going to keep him up all night. *Beep.* Jeremy could see a little bit of light coming from under the curtain, just like he could see light peeking through the bottom of his bedroom door at home when the hallway light was on. Not a lot of light: just a little. *Beep.* He closed his eyes and listened to the sound of the nurses' shoes clacking up and down the hallway. When the footsteps sounded like they were coming close, he opened his eyes, hoping that a nurse was bringing him something to eat. *Beep.* Alas, no one came into his curtained-off room with a snack.

Jeremy's recollection as to what happened next was cloudy. For starters, he was unsure if he fell asleep or remained awake. When he later tried to reconstruct the details of that night's events, Jeremy wasn't sure he could tell the difference between what *actually* occurred in the hospital room and what may have only occurred in a dream. At home, he usually had dreams that were in color and sometimes they could be very realistic. Every once in a while, Jeremy woke up and wasn't immediately sure if the events that occurred in his dream were actually real-world events. After a minute, he would figure out that the floor of his bedroom was *not* lava. *Beep.* Jeremy turned his head away from the curtain and looked out the window. He had a vivid recollection of looking out over the visitor parking lot and noticing that there were very few cars remaining. A big dog, possibly a Labrador Retriever, ran across the parking lot, and Jeremy wondered if someone had lost their dog or if it was a stray. All the while in the background, he still heard the beeping machine.

He thought to himself, "I wonder what time it is?" For no good reason, he became pre-occupied with the time. He looked around the room but he couldn't find a clock.

"Eleven o'clock," a voice from the far end of the room said. "Do you know where your children are?"

There was a surprised yelp in the back of Jeremy's throat but no sound came out of his mouth. Instead, he let out a rush of air from between his lips like he was trying to blow out candles on a birthday cake. It was an adult's voice and it came from a shadowy corner at the far end of Jeremy's hospital room. Jeremy lifted his head off the pillow and peered into the darkness beyond the foot of his bed. His pupils enlarged, letting in as much light as possible. He sat up as much as his bindings permitted and squinted his eyes, but he couldn't see anything lurking in the corner of his room.

Suddenly, the stabbing pain in his belly returned and his head fell backward onto his pillow. It felt like someone had stuck a knife into his belly and was twisting it. The suddenness and severity of the pain caused Jeremy to lose his breath. He opened his mouth wide but sound didn't come out and air didn't come in.

There was a smacking sound of leather dress shoes on the linoleum floor as a man in a dark business suit walked out of the corner of his hospital room. "I've been watching you for a long time," he said. "A very long time indeed." The man spoke calmly and warmly.

Jeremy couldn't speak nor move. It felt as though the rubber tubing snaking down behind his tonsils had become much wider, closing off most of his airway. He could only manage to take little baby sips of air.

"You have certain, how shall I say it?" the man pulled from his suit jacket a pack of cigarettes and tapped it against his other hand so that a single cigarette popped up out of the pack. "You have *special qualities*. Qualities that we are looking for," the man said, placing the cigarette in his mouth. While holding the unlit cigarette between his lips, he repeated himself, as if he was reaffirming what he'd just said. "Mmmm huh: qualities."

The man walked up to the foot of Jeremy's bed and took out a silver metal lighter from his suit jacket pocket. "You may not realize it but you are special," he said, walking to the side of Jeremy's bed. He was close enough that Jeremy could smell the butane coming from the lighter as he flicked it open and ignited the flame. After he lit his cigarette, the man casually flipped the lighter shut. The first drag that the man took of the cigarette was long and deep, causing the end of the cigarette to glow intensely. The man exhaled the smoke directly at Jeremy so that it engulfed him. Jeremy had smelled cigarettes before, even though neither of his parents smoked. Instead of the acrid smell that Jeremy was expecting, the smoke smelled a little like a pumpkin pie that had just been pulled out of the oven.

In the light created by the orange tip of the lit cigarette, Jeremy saw that the man looked very relaxed. The left side of his mouth was just a little higher than the right, creating a faint, sarcastic looking smile. During the silence, the man flipped the metallic lighter open and then shut a few times, which made a sharp snapping noise. The man looked down at Jeremy as he repeatedly snapped his lighter open and shut in a steady rhythm. Jeremy's throat relaxed enough that he was able to say in a barely audible voice, "No."

"No what?" the man said, looking as though he was taken aback. "That's not a very nice thing to say. What are you saying 'no' to? You don't even know what I'm talking about yet."

Once again, Jeremy summoned his courage and once again softly said, "No."

"Why are you being so petulant?" the man asked, using the lit cigarette in his hand to point at Jeremy.

Jeremy had no idea what *petulant* meant. He wanted to ask what that word meant but since he was still only able to take little sips of air, Jeremy just shook his head in defiance.

"This is certainly not the way I wanted our relationship to begin, Jeremy," remarked the man in the dark businessman's suit as he turned his back on Jeremy and walked back towards the foot of the bed. He had almost reached the dark corner of the room from which he emerged when he said, "But, if that's how you want it…"

The head of Jeremy's bed suddenly jerked upward so that the bed was nearly at a right angle to the floor. Jeremy hung from his tethered wrists and he watched in horror as the tiled floor at the foot of the bed cracked and then opened up, revealing a deep maw. The large pitch black hole at the foot of his bed was as big as a twin mattress and Jeremy was poised to slide down into its depths. Jeremy kicked frantically with his bare feet, trying to scramble up towards the head of the bed but all he accomplished was to kick the sheet and blanket off the foot of the bed. He watched the sheet and blanket fluttering down the dark chasm and then out of sight. But for the wrist restraints tethering him to the bed's side rails, Jeremy was sure that he'd slide down the bed's steep incline and into the hole. Even though the restraints were keeping him from falling off the slanted bed for the time being, Jeremy didn't know how long they could keep him from plunging into the gaping chasm. Mom had gently but firmly tied the restraints, but there was no telling how long they could keep him from sliding down the bed and into the pit.

A vicious spasm in the lower part of Jeremy's belly caused him to gasp. With lungs now full of air, Jeremy let out a loud cry of pain. Each time there was a spasm, it felt like a red hot poker had skewered his groin and lower abdomen. Each spasm caused him to gasp in pain, filling his lungs with air. Now that he had regained his breath, he screamed with agony and fear every time one of those spasms ripped through his belly.

When Nasty Nurse rushed into the room, Jeremy's bed was once again on its four posts. "What the hell is going on in here?" she shrieked, flipping on the light switch.

Jeremy looked towards the foot of his bed but the chasm and the man in the dark suit were gone. He was drenched in cold sweat, as if someone had dumped a large bucket of ice water over him. The last thing that Jeremy remembered was crying out and pulling his knees to his chest because his guts hurt so badly.

CHAPTER FOUR

A Little Bowel Surgery

Jeremy awoke slowly, as he yo-yoed in and out of consciousness. Sunlight was streaming through the window. His parents were on either side of his hospital bed. When he tried to speak, he noticed that his tongue felt fat and that there was absolutely no spit in his mouth. Jeremy tried to say something to his mother, but someone had apparently dumped sand into his mouth. All he could manage was to make a soft "*kack*" sound with his dry mouth.

"Water? Do you want a drink of water?" his mother asked, and his father quickly fumbled with a plastic carafe of water and a Styrofoam cup.

Although he'd never been as thirsty as he was at that moment, it ended up being the most disappointing glass of water that he ever drank. The small cup of cool water did absolutely nothing to make his mouth moist or quench his thirst. Jeremy pointed at the container for more but his mother said, "Sorry, honey, you can only have a little to drink. We have to go slow. You had surgery, honey."

He was old enough to know what surgery was but he still gave his mother a childlike look of incomprehension. Electric impulses fired through his awakening brain. His brain's telephone switchboard was being inundated with frantic inquiries, most of which were asking, "What happened to us?!" Slowly, Jeremy's young brain began to take inventory of the situation. He was experiencing a dull but strong ache in his stomach. Jeremy lifted up his head and looked down to see that there was a large pillow of gauze covering his lower abdomen. In addition, there was a small clear piece of tubing coming from under the gauze with clearish/yellowish fluid in it. He was thankful when he noticed that the brown rubber tube was no longer threaded through his nose and down the back of his throat. However, his throat now hurt much worse than it had when the tube had been in place. His mouth and throat felt puffy, dry and *beaten up,* as if the whole area had been scrubbed with coarse sandpaper.

During the following six days he spent in the hospital, Jeremy overheard enough conversations among the adults to learn that when he was in the emergency room, his guts (also called your *bowel*) had a small obstruction, which the brown tube down his throat was somehow supposed to fix. When he started feeling better the following afternoon, this was a sign that the small bowel obstruction was going away. Another problem with his bowel, however, developed the night he was visited by the man in the dark suit. The doctor told his parents that Jeremy's bowel twisted later that night and this led to him being rushed into an operating room for emergency surgery to untangle his bowel.

The sharp pain had mercifully gone away, leaving just a dull ache in his belly and groin that was much more tolerable. The searing spasms of burning pain that he had when the man in the suit visited him were the worst he had ever felt and he hoped the surgery made it so that pain never came back. A few days after the surgery he was at last permitted to eat, although he was started off with just broth and pudding.

It was odd that the doctors, nurses, and his parents were very focused on Jeremy needing to poop over the following days. Every nurse and doctor who came into his room asked him, "Have you pooped yet?" Whenever he shifted in the bed to get comfortable, one of his parents usually asked, "Do you feel like you need to go to the bathroom?" On the fourth day, Jeremy pooped, and he was amazed at how happy this made everybody. Mom and dad acted like he'd just thrown a touchdown in a championship game! Jeremy didn't understand what the big deal was. It was just a poop, for heaven's sake!

After the surgery and before he was discharged from the hospital, Jeremy had vivid dreams every night. For the most part, they were the typical type of dreams that he had back home. Most of them were just weird and didn't make much sense. Sometimes he awoke with only fragmented recollections of his dreams. All of his dreams in the hospital were full of frantic activity. One night, he was in a row boat with three other people and they were all trying to keep the leaky boat from sinking. In another dream, a cake was sitting on the kitchen table and when it suddenly blew apart, Jeremy and his friends were trying to pick up all of the pieces and put the cake back together before his parents saw the huge mess.

Jeremy was very happy when he was told by his father that he was going to be sent home the next morning. He had a hard time going to sleep on his last night in the hospital because he was so excited to get home. Going back to school was a cakewalk compared to undergoing abdominal surgery! His mid-section was still tender and he walked a little hunched over like an old man. Mom said she would make him his favorite supper on the evening that he was discharged. Just the thought of roast beef, mashed potatoes, and orange Jell-o with shredded carrots in it was enough to make Jeremy's mouth water.

On his last night in the hospital, Jeremy dreamt that a tornado was coming. He could see a swirling gray vortex hovering above the neighborhood on a direct collision course with his family's house. The tornado sirens were blaring but instead of bellowing out a strong, single note, they were playing music. It sounded like a jazz musician was trying to play as many notes as possible on his trumpet without stopping. The odd tornado alarm wasn't the only unusual thing in his dream. For some reason his family was living in a tall pink house that had green flowers painted on the sides of it. He and his parents were on their knees in the garden, trying to pick the vegetables so that they'd have something to eat once they had taken refuge in the basement.

"Let's go! We got to take cover!" his father yelled over the free-form, jazz odyssey blaring from the sirens.

As he raced towards the house with his hands full of tomatoes, Jeremy saw a man in a dark business suit watching them from the neighbor's yard. The man stood quietly and showed no emotion. As his parents ran into the house, the screen door slamming behind them, Jeremy stopped and looked at the man. Despite the fact that a strong wind was whipping around, the man appeared to be unaffected and his crisply pressed black suit did not move. His mother called his name from the door, which broke Jeremy's fascination with the man in the dark suit. Jeremy ran into the house and followed his mother down into the basement. It was there that Jeremy, his parents and the four members of The Monkees ate ice cream and tomatoes until the storm had passed. Just as Davy Jones asked for more ice cream, Jeremy woke up. He was in the hospital room, but neither his parents nor The Monkees were anywhere in sight.

From the time of surgery until the dream he had that last night in the hospital, Jeremy hadn't remembered his encounter with the man in the dark suit. Seeing him standing in their neighbor's yard during the storm however brought back all the details of his short conversation with the man the night of his surgery. He had had so many vivid dreams since the emergency surgery, Jeremy figured that the whole incident with the man in the dark suit and the gaping chasm at the foot of his bed were just part of a crazy dream. As he lay in the hospital bed and thought intently about the encounter, he remembered details that didn't seem like they were part of a dream. Such things as smelling the butane lighter and the odd pumpkin pie smoke from the cigarette seemed too real to just be part of a dream. The bright glow of the cigarette in the shadowy hospital room seemed real, not make-believe. These were very specific details of the sort that he didn't remember having in *any* of his other dreams, even the wild and vivid ones.

Jeremy pushed the call light and was pleased when Nice Nurse arrived about a minute later. He explained in detail what he could remember about his encounter with the man in the dark suit on the night of his surgery and the nurse listened patiently. He told her about the gaping hole that had opened at the foot his bed. Once he'd shared with her all of the information that he could remember, she patted him on the hand and advised, "You just need your sleep. Shush now and go to sleep. Tomorrow is a big day for this big man!" Jeremy blushed. Despite wanting to talk some more with the love of his life, he was indeed tired and he nodded off quickly.

CHAPTER FIVE

The Secret Club

Just as planned, Jeremy went home the next day. When he returned to school, he spent a significant amount of his first day telling several of his classmates and his teacher about his ordeal. Although he was still a little run down, Jeremy felt good. He was happy to be back in his old routine. His teacher seemed to be a little nicer to him than usual, so that was a welcome change of pace. He was so focused on getting back to school and making up his assignments, he forgot about the dreams in the hospital and the two encounters he had with the man in the dark suit.

Once he was home, he continued to have vivid dreams, but he couldn't recall if the man in the dark suit made any cameo appearances. After a week at home, he was for the most part back to normal, except for the big surgical scar running down his abdomen. He was hesitant to show anyone the long surgical scar since it ended kind of close to his groin. After school one day, however, he pulled up his shirt to show his two best friends the raised pink scar than ran down his lower abdomen. His friends were amazed at how big the scar was and told Jeremy that they were surprised that *anyone* could survive such a massive surgical wound.

On Friday of his first week back at school, all the kids were pleased when their teacher announced that they were going to watch a film strip. Jeremy thought that this would be a nice change of pace from listening to the teacher's prattle. She put a record on the phonograph and an authoritative male voice narrated the film strip. When there was a *beep* on the record, the teacher turned the crank on the filmstrip machine to show the next image. *Beep.* The door to the classroom was closed so that other classes wouldn't be disturbed by the narrator's booming voice. Watching the filmstrip, Jeremy felt a twinge in his belly and absently put his hand over the area of his incision. From the corner of his eye, Jeremy saw movement, as if someone had been in the hallway looking through the window into the classroom and then ran away. *Beep.* He turned his head away from the image projected on the screen at the front of the classroom and looked at the door. *Beep.* On either side of the door was a six-inch strip of safety glass through which you could look into or out of the classroom. Jeremy's eyes darted over to the windows to the left and right of the classroom door, but he saw nothing. *Beep.*

The teacher cleared her throat and Jeremy turned his attention back to the filmstrip. Shortly, however, he once again detected a flash of movement in the corner of his eye. Something dark. This time Jeremy quickly twisted his head as soon as he detected movement. *Beep.* Still lightly rubbing his abdomen, Jeremy gazed intently at the windows that framed the classroom door. When he was satisfied that there was nothing to see, he began to turn his head back towards the screen. *Beep.* Just as he did so, he saw what looked like a tall, dark figure rush past the windows. He felt a sudden cramp, as if someone had reached into his belly and squeezed a handful of his guts. The pain went away after just a few seconds, but it was sudden and strong enough to cause Jeremy to wince.

Jeremy abruptly leapt from his desk and ran to the door. In one swift motion, he turned the doorknob and slammed his shoulder against the door, which caused him to spill out of the classroom and onto the hallway floor. From his seat on the floor, he could see down both directions of the long hallway. Quickly, he snapped his head to the left and then to the right, expecting to see something or someone in the hallway. Nobody was there.

"What do you think you're doing, Jeremy?" the teacher squawked, towering above her student.

Jeremy stopped checking the hallways and looked up. "I...I thought I saw something. Someone."

She lifted him off the floor by grabbing the back of his shirt. "Principal Wohlers' office. Now!"

Jeremy shuffled slowly towards the principal's office. It was a walk of shame that he'd never made before that day. Jeremy thought about the intense interrogation that surely was waiting for him by the principal. He'd been told horror stories about what happens when you were sent to the principal's office. Even if you assumed that at least half of the stuff you heard was made-up, Jeremy was nervous. What could he say to the principal? He had no good explanation for what he'd just done. Certainly he wasn't going to tell the principal about the dark-suited man who first visited him in his hospital room and how Jeremy thought that the man may have been skulking around outside of his classroom. There was no way that he was going to tell the principal that he felt oddly compelled to run to the door and investigate.

The slow walk to the principal's office gave Jeremy enough time to come up with a plausible reason for his actions. Jeremy told the principal that he thought he had seen someone in the hallway who didn't look like he belonged in the school. He admitted that he acted rashly and that he should have alerted his teacher that there might be a stranger in the hallway as opposed to darting out of the classroom. Recognizing that Jeremy had been through a lot over the past few weeks and that he had no previous misdeeds, Principal Wohlers had him sit in his office for awhile to let things settle down. In the principal's opinion, Jeremy's impulsive act didn't warrant a phone call to his parents or any other intervention. After he was assured that the storm had passed, Principal Wohlers sent Jeremy back to the classroom with a stern warning for him not to repeat the act.

When Jeremy slept that night, he dreamt he was being chased. He didn't know who or what his pursuer was, just that he desperately needed to escape its clutches. As he ran, his legs became progressively heavier and eventually, he was paralyzed below the waist. After falling, Jeremy used his hands to drag himself along the ground. A fierce spasm of pain erupted in his belly. He pictured in his mind that his guts were long tubes which were being twisted into the shape of a balloon animal. He grabbed big handfuls of dirt and grass, trying to pull himself away from his pursuer. Jeremy took a moment to look behind him but he still couldn't see what was chasing him. There was no doubt in Jeremy's mind, though, that someone or something evil was still after him and that he needed to get away.

Jeremy turned his head and looked forward. As soon as he did, he was looking at the bottom of two pants legs. He looked up and saw that it was a man's legs. Jeremy saw that it was not *a* man: it was *the* man. The man was once again wearing his nicely pressed black business suit and was using his lips to hold a lit cigarette in the corner of his mouth. While still holding the cigarette between his lips, the man said, "Long time, no see. Ready to talk?"

Jeremy looked back over his shoulder, but he still couldn't see his pursuer. He shifted his weight and started to drag himself to the left of the legs, but the man moved his foot so that it was once again in front of Jeremy.

"You know, I can help you," the man said. When Jeremy tried to pull himself to the right, the man once again moved his leg to block the path.

Jeremy felt as though his inexplicable paralysis was moving up his body and was starting to invade the muscles in his arms. With each passing moment, his arms were growing weaker. Pretty soon he would be helpless, lying on the ground and defenselessly waiting to be caught.

"With what?" Jeremy asked, his arms becoming so weak that they buckled, causing him to fall to the ground.

The man squatted down in front of the boy. "With *everything*, of course!" he said with a big smile.

Jeremy could smell the man's cigarette smoke, but this time it smelled like burnt peanut butter cookies.

"Let's get away from here," the man said from his crouching position in front of Jeremy. "We don't need him hanging around." Just like he'd done in the hospital room, the man used his lit cigarette as a pointer, directing the lit end towards the area behind Jeremy. Jeremy looked back over his shoulder and saw a glowing yellow blob slowly moving towards the two of them. It was the monster that Jeremy had seen on an episode of *Johnny Quest*. The monster had a menacing, gaping maw, and it began to shriek.

Over the monster's loud screech, Jeremy heard what sounded like handfuls of crispy potato chips being crushed all around him. He looked away from the monster and saw that the ground he was lying on was cracking. As the monster moved closer, the cracking sound intensified, and fissures opened in the ground. Jeremy turned his head and saw that the monster was only a few feet away. It was then that Jeremy heard the crash of breaking glass. The ground under Jeremy broke open, and he was in a free fall. No longer paralyzed, Jeremy's arms and legs flailed in the air as he fell.

The end of his descent was sudden but soft. Jeremy found himself seated in an overstuffed high-back chair like the kind that his grandfather kept in his study. He looked around him and was surprised when he didn't see any debris or broken glass. There was likewise no dirt or glass on Jeremy's jeans or sweatshirt. Jeremy looked above him from where he'd fallen but only saw an ordinary white ceiling. As far as Jeremy could tell, he was seated comfortably in what looked like a set taken from the old Batman television show Jeremy watched reruns of on Saturday mornings. The Bat-Computer consisted of flimsy cardboard props with crudely painted details. On the desk next to Jeremy's chair was the bright red Bat-Phone that linked the caped crusader directly to the chief of police. The man in the dark suit was casually sitting on the end of the desk with his ankles crossed and a sly, satisfied smile on his face.

"That's better, don't you think, Jeremy?" said the man.

"You know my name?"

The man snorted loudly. "Of course I do. Like I told you, I've been watching you for quite some time."

In Jeremy's experience, it was typically at about this point in a dream that things would become confused and silly. A dream might begin with you casually talking to your mother about what you wanted for Christmas and then she'd suddenly become a bird and fly away. Jeremy waited patiently for the scene to morph into something that did not make sense. Scanning the room, he wasn't going to be surprised if the Batcave turned into a circus midway with calliope music playing. Or change into a school assembly that Jeremy had inexplicably decided to attend naked.

After a prolonged silence, the man quipped, "Cat got your tongue, Jeremy?"

"Who are you?" Jeremy asked and then for some reason immediately asked the question a second time, this time a little louder.

The man in the dark suit retrieved his pack of cigarettes and prepared to light up. "You can call me Mr. Daymo. Do you think you can remember that? It kind of sounds like, 'It's a good *day* to *mow* the lawn.' Got it?"

"What does that mean?"

"It's just a name. You asked for my name, and I gave it to you. Would you prefer if I said that my name was Mr. Shoe? Mr. Dark

Suit Guy? How about Felicity the horse riding impresario?"

"What's an impr…impre…?"

The man chuckled a little and said, "Let me ask you this, smart guy: what does *Jeremy* mean? Or *Jeremy Bracken* for that matter? Hmmm? What does that name mean?"

"I don't know," Jeremy responded meekly.

Mr. Daymo slapped his thigh with his hand. "Well, then, why are you asking about the meaning of my name? It looks like we're in the same boat: neither of us know the historical or cosmic significance of our names. I guess that means that we have yet something else in common, my young friend."

Still expecting the scene to change into something else, Jeremy took a quick glance around the room, but everything remained the same.

Mr. Daymo stopped smiling and looked intently at Jeremy. "We don't have lots of time together, and there's a lot of ground that we need to cover. To make this process go smoother, let me explain to you our basic ground rules."

There was something in Mr. Daymo's voice that concerned Jeremy. His tone had gone quickly from friendly banter to the kind of voice used by adults when they were about to give you important information. The man pointed the lit end of his cigarette at Jeremy.

"Truth be known, you have already broken an important rule, young man. It is *very* important that no one know about me. No one. You and I are members of a secret club. No girls, boys or adults allowed inside! Just the two of us old cowboys! Is that absolutely clear?" Jeremy nodded his head, too scared to speak. "You've already broken that rule, haven't you? You told that pretty hospital nurse about our first meeting, do you remember?"

Jeremy had no recollection of talking to anyone about the man in the dark suit, so he replied honestly, "No, I haven't told nobody."

"Well, you did, buckaroo. As a result, that caused me to have to *take care of her,*" he said, crushing out his half smoked cigarette in a Bat-Ashtray that was on the Bat-Desk, as if he was emphasizing his point.

"What…what do you mean?"

"Never you mind right now. Just remember that if you tell anyone about me, bad things will happen to both you and them. I'm letting you off the hook this time because the rules hadn't been made clear to you. I can assure you, my young friend, that was your one and only mulligan."

"What's a mulligan?"

"It's a type of soup. The important thing for you to remember is that there can be dire consequences to your actions. You do know what *dire circumstances* means, right?" Jeremy nodded his head. "Sure you do! For example, let's take the dire circumstances that occurred because you decided to gorge yourself on Halloween candy?"

"What about the candy?" Jeremy asked, feeling a little defensive.

"That's why you got a bowel obstruction and ended up with a twisted bowel that required emergency surgery."

"But my parents and the doctor said I didn't cause that. They said that the candy had nothing to do with it. They used a long word to describe it. *Sarandilly* or something like that. "

"Of course they told you it was serendipity. They didn't want you blaming yourself for the whole ordeal," Mr. Daymo said. He tapped his temple with his forefinger and added, "That degree of guilt is usually considered not healthy for the developing brain of a kid. But I am telling you that the sooner you realize that all of your actions have real world repercussions, the better off you'll be."

Jeremy was all of a sudden defiant and a little hurt that he was being blamed for his hospitalization and surgery. "Who are you to say that? Are you a doctor?"

Mr. Daymo tucked his chin down towards his chest, a little surprised by the kid's spirit. "You know I'm not a doctor," he said, gesturing towards his dark clothing. "Do I look like a doctor?"

"Then what *are* you?"

The man raised his eyebrows. He had to admit to himself that he was a little impressed with how the boy was handling himself.

"A fine question from a fine young man," Mr. Daymo said with a false jovial tone in his voice. "But it's not one that can be easily answered. Let's just say that you... are under my tutelage. You will learn that for every force, there is a corresponding opposite force. For every day, there is night. For every laugh, there is a tear."

Jeremy looked up at Mr. Daymo with a confused look on his young face.

"In time, we will deal with all that." Mr. Daymo looked at his watch. "Unfortunately, we're about out of time tonight. Quickly before I leave: who do you tell about The Secret Club?"

"Nobody," Jeremy replied.

Mr. Daymo once again slapped his thigh with his hand. "That's my boy!"

All of the room's cardboard walls fell backwards. Jeremy and Mr. Daymo were in the vacant lot down the street from the school where Jeremy and his friends sometimes played. The man in the dark suit melted into a blob and then became a white horse who trotted off in the opposite direction. Jeremy looked down and saw that he was sitting on a wooden fence. He was wearing cowboy clothes except he was wearing pink furry slippers instead of boots. The dream got sillier and sillier from there.

CHAPTER SIX

The Mr. Daymo Show

From that point, Jeremy saw Mr. Daymo every night in his dreams. There were times that Mr. Daymo was just watching Jeremy, like he did in the dream where he was standing in their neighbor's yard while the tornado approached. Other times, Mr. Daymo spoke directly with Jeremy. Every time Mr. Daymo appeared in his dreams, Jeremy experienced a painful twinge in his belly. Most of the time, Mr. Daymo showed up right after the pain occurred. If Mr. Daymo didn't immediately appear after the pain hit, Jeremy looked around, trying to find where the man in the dark suit was lurking. Although the man might just appear in the dream for a short time, Jeremy always eventually found him and locked eyes with him before waking up.

The Mister Daymo Show became Jeremy's nightly entertainment. The show was unpredictable and would run the gamut of being bizarre, exciting, scary, or funny. No two shows were alike. Jeremy played kickball with the Harlem Globetrotters. He got into a fist fight with Captain Crunch over a dispute as to whether crunch berries should be in his cereal. He fell helplessly from high places and was pursued by monsters on several occasions. Jeremy once saw Nice Nurse as she was riding a bicycle through snowdrifts. She was still wearing her white uniform, and she was still beautiful.

One night, Jeremy dreamt that he was at school, seated at his desk. Looking around him, he saw that all of the other desks were occupied by people he didn't immediately recognize. As he looked more carefully, he realized that a store mannequin was seated at each desk. No two mannequins looked the same. Some of them didn't have heads and others didn't have arms. Jeremy's attention was drawn to the torso of a woman that was perched on a desk wearing nothing but a white bra. Jeremy was unnerved by the collection of silent plastic classmates and tried to get up from his desk. He couldn't move, the seat of his pants seemingly stuck to the chair. It was as if Jeremy had sat in the biggest, stickiest wad of gum and his butt was firmly glued to the chair. When he tried to move the rest of his body, it felt like his shoes were welded to the floor and his folded hands were super-glued to the top of his desk. Trying to jerk his hands and feet from their moorings had no effect: they were stuck. A sudden gripping pain in his stomach caused Jeremy to wince, and he lowered his head down onto his two folded hands stuck to the desktop as he gritted his teeth.

"Stop squirming, Jeremy," someone said. Jeremy lifted his head and saw his teacher standing at the blackboard. She still had her trademark large red bouffant hairdo but her face had been replaced with Mr. Daymo's. "It's time to learn, not fool around," Teacher Daymo said, taking a pack of cigarettes out of the teacher's desk. Jeremy tried once again to free himself from the desk, but it became clear that any such efforts were pointless.

"Are you done yet?" Teacher Daymo asked in a sinister tone, lighting a cigarette with a silver metal flip lighter. Jeremy stopped fussing and turned his attention to the teacher. Since he was glued to the desk with his folded hands on the desk top, Jeremy was the epitome of what an "A" student looked like.

"Good. It's time to learn," Teacher Daymo announced. The classroom lights dimmed and a filmstrip projector turned itself on. Teacher Daymo pulled down a white projection screen and gingerly put the arm of a phonograph on a record.

The voice coming from the phonograph was very deep and

sounded quite serious. "Today's lesson. An overview." On the projection screen were the words "Overview for Jeremy".

Teacher Daymo sat down on the edge of the teacher's desk and watched the presentation while tapping her cigarette ashes onto the floor of the classroom. The voice on the record advised, "When you hear the tone, turn the filmstrip to the next image. Do so now. *Beep.*" The film projector moved to the next slide on its own. A black and white photograph of man standing stiffly appeared on the screen. He was dressed in an ornate military uniform with a row of medals pinned to his chest. Because his left arm was missing, the sleeve had been carefully folded and the cuff was pinned to his shoulder. "Amputation. Service," the voice on the record said. *Beep.* A photo of a black child with a large protruding belly was shown. "Starvation. Famine." *Beep.* Another photograph, this one of a woman bent backwards and being held by a man wearing a sailor's uniform. They were kissing while standing on a very busy city street. "Desire. Victory. Elation." *Beep.*

The presentation of images and words started off slowly but the pace quickly increased to the point that each of the filmstrip images was only on the screen for a second or two. The narrator on the record spoke faster to keep up with the torrid pace of the images. A man with funny little black mustache appeared on the screen. "Dictator. Annihilation. Genocide." *Beep.* A drawing of a guillotine. "Revolution. Beheading. Execution." *Beep.* A photo of a mother holding a baby. "Absolute devotion. Nurture." Jeremy couldn't remember how long this presentation went on, but when he woke up the next morning, his eyes were overly sensitive to light for most of the day. While at school, he often had to use his hand to shade his eyes. Try as he might, he wasn't able to remember exactly what words he heard or what images he had been shown.

In another dream, Jeremy was in a huge library. One by one, books flew off the shelves and pelted him. When the books hit him, it didn't hurt as much as being hit with a baseball, but it felt hard enough that he was concerned that he was going to be covered with bruises. Librarian Daymo watched the onslaught from the circulation desk with a satisfied grin on his face. When Jeremy used his hands to cover his face, the books hit him in the chest. When he curled up in a ball, the books slammed into his back. When Jeremy woke up, he quickly pulled up his pajama shirt and inspected himself. He didn't have any welts where the books hit him, and he never developed any bruises in the days that followed.

One night shortly before Christmas, Jeremy dreamt he was seated on the lap of Santa Claus in the middle of a shopping mall that Jeremy didn't immediately recognize. Initially, it was a pleasant dream where Jeremy was telling St. Nicholas of all the things that he hoped would be waiting for him under the tree. Before he was done telling the round-faced man what he wanted, a sudden stabbing cramp wrenched the boy's lower abdomen. When Jeremy looked back at Santa, his face had changed. Even though the lower part of his face was covered in a fake white beard, Jeremy knew immediately that he was now sitting on the lap of Santa Daymo.

Without announcing that he had taken over the body of jolly bearded man, Santa Daymo reached inside his thick, fuzzy red and white coat. Pulling out a pack of cigarettes, he abruptly said, "So, my friend, let's get down to brass tacks."

"To brass what?"

"We need to ramp up the process. You see, you're like a small green tomato on the vine and I need you to become mature enough that you can be harvested." Jeremy thought that tomatoes seemed to be part of a disproportionate number of his dreams lately. He wondered why that was so. "You need to get prepared and ready to go."

"Ready for what?"

Santa Daymo furrowed his brow and looked down on the

boy. "For what you've been chosen to do. Haven't you been paying attention for the past month?" Santa Daymo's tone was very accusatory. Jeremy's eyes got wide, and he pictured himself being dropped to the ground by the large fake Santa. Jeremy figured that it would be in his best interest to say *yes*, so he did so.

"Good. Remember: this is for your benefit as much as it is for mine." As Santa Daymo lit his cigarette, Jeremy smelled what seemed to be a combination of a number of different exotic plants, none of which he could specifically identify. As a cloud of cigarette smoke engulfed the two, Jeremy looked around and noticed that everyone else in the mall's Christmas display was frozen in place like they were statues.

When Jeremy looked again into the face of the festively disguised Mr. Daymo, the fake Santa glared at Jeremy. From the look on his face, it appeared as if Santa Daymo was expecting the boy to say something. Jeremy wasn't sure what he was supposed to say or do. Jeremy tried hard to remember if Santa Daymo had asked him a question before he lit his cigarette. Jeremy felt he needed to say *something*. Hesitantly, Jeremy said, "So, you were talking about the brass taxes and the unripe green tomatoes: what do you want me to do with them?"

The bearded man sighed and brought his face down to Jeremy's so that their noses were almost touching. "When we're together, your one and only task is to listen and learn. Well, I guess that's actually two tasks. Task number one is to listen and task number two is to learn. Got it? Don't close your eyes. Don't start blubbering. And for heaven's sake, don't start running around flailing your arms like you are a stupid girl in a horror movie. Capeesh?"

Jeremy understood everything he said until the last word but he simply nodded in agreement. Jolly St. Daymo pulled his face back from the boy and reached down to the floor to grab a placard that was propped against his chair. In chalk, someone had written,

"See Santa Claus. All day today." Santa Daymo wiped his white gloved hand over the slate, smearing the chalk. After a couple passes of his glove, the placard became a small television screen. "Watch this," St. Daymo instructed, pointing the lit end of his cigarette at the screen.

When Jeremy looked at the screen, he was immediately transported out of the mall. Instead of looking at a little TV screen, he was standing in a huge movie theater where the screen was wrapped completely around him. There were no seats in this theater, just Jeremy, standing in the middle of a theater where the projection screen formed a circle. While the screen was still black, a voice thundered in a language that Jeremy didn't understand. It was clear from the speaker's inflection that what was being said was *very* important. A series of images started to flash on the screen in fast succession. When Jeremy tried to think about what he'd just seen, the image was quickly replaced with another photographic image. All the while, the booming voice was giving furtive commands. As Jeremy's senses were being inundated with flashing images and the loud soundtrack, he began to feel dizzy and disoriented. He reached for something to grab onto but found nothing, so he stumbled to the side a few steps and bumped into the screen. The voice got louder and the sequence of pictures got faster, causing Jeremy's head to spin even faster. He closed his eyes but he could still see the images because they somehow passed through his eyelids.

"Stop!" Jeremy yelled. "Stop!" The crazy movie kept going, and he only managed to get momentary relief from the rapid succession of images by covering his eyes with his hand. The voice bellowing from the unseen speakers barked an even louder command, and Jeremy felt a little electrical shock on the hand that was covering his eyes. Although the shock wasn't very painful, it surprised him and he let out a *yelp*. When he pulled his hand away, the images were even more colorful and vibrant, causing Jeremy to squint his eyes. "Stop! Stop! Stop!" he commanded, holding his outstretched hands towards the screen.

After Jeremy yelled "Stop!" for what seemed the hundredth time, the screen turned into a blinding white light. Jeremy closed his eyes tightly as the light enveloped him. When he cautiously opened his eyes, he was looking into the face of his mother, who was gently shaking him. "Wake up, honey. It's just a nightmare," she soothed. When her son looked confused, she explained in a loving voice, "It's alright, honey. It's not real. You're here with me. Nothing is going to hurt you." Jeremy lunged at his mother and buried his sweaty forehead into the nape of her neck. "Shhhhhh, it's okay, little man. It's all okay," she said, stroking his hair. Once he was given a minute to get his bearings, she was right: he *was* okay. After drinking a small glass of water and being tucked back in, Jeremy gazed at the ceiling and wondered if it was going to turn into a movie screen. Jeremy was a little hesitant to close his eyes but when he did, he was treated to calm, restful and dreamless sleep for the remainder of the night.

At the kitchen table the next morning, his father asked, "What did you dream about last night?"

Jeremy thought about the previous night and had a vivid recollection of sitting on the lap of Santa Daymo. He was about to blurt out something about dreaming that he was with Santa Claus but he caught himself. Since he'd been sternly warned that bad things happen when little boys talk, he figured that it was probably best to just say nothing. Jeremy tried to give his dad a casual smile and replied, "I can't remember now, Dad."

His father chuckled a little and said, "It must've been a pretty nasty monster that was chasing you! You were talking and yelling in your sleep loud enough that you woke up both me and your mom!" His father took one last drink of coffee from his mug and then got up from the kitchen table. "Gotta go. The bus has been running a little early lately." He ruffled his son's hair and said, "Have a good day, sport." As his father did so, his cologne wafted in the air and Jeremy smelled the scent of several exotic plants. Jeremy's stomach tightened. The cologne smelled a lot like the scent that came from Santa Daymo's cigarette. Jeremy cringed from his father's touch. "Dad! What is that smell?" he asked in a concerned and wary tone.

"What? Oh, you mean my new cologne? Do you like it?"

Jeremy wrinkled his nose and put his left hand on his abdomen. "No! *Ech!* It makes my stomach hurt. What *is* it?"

"It's called *Hai Karate*. The commercial says that it smells so good that you'll have to use karate to keep the pretty girls away!" his dad said with bravado. He made a cartoonish karate chop in the air and playfully yelled *"Heeyah!"*

Jeremy's mom giggled and blew a flirty kiss to her husband. He winked at her and she returned the wink.

On the last day of school before Christmas break, all of the students and teachers had for the most part already checked-out for the holiday. Both the students and the teachers thought fondly of the upcoming holiday and the prospect of sleeping late. There was one kid, however, who wasn't focused on playing in the snow and unwrapping gifts. Jeremy spent the last day of school trying desperately to remember what he'd seen in the wraparound theater. He must have been shown a thousand images on the screen but no matter how much he concentrated, he couldn't remember a single one. All he could remember was that there was a blur of pictures that were flashed on the huge movie screen. As the clock moved agonizingly slow that afternoon, Jeremy turned his thoughts to the voice that had been broadcast in the cavernous theater. He was confident that what he heard wasn't English, but that was as far as Jeremy's analysis could go. How could he go about finding out what language it was when he couldn't recognize it or remember what was said? When he got home after school, he asked his mother how many languages she could speak and she told him that she only knew one.

"How many different languages are there?" he asked his mother.

"You mean in the whole wide world?" she asked.

"Yeah, how many different ones are there?"

"Oh, I don't know. I guess hundreds. Thousands, even. There's a lot, but that's about all I can tell you, honey."

Jeremy did his best to delay his bedtime that night. After his encounter with Santa Daymo, he was apprehensive about going to sleep. The scary experience in the theater was very unpleasant and he wasn't looking forward to going through it again. He wasn't sure if a repeat performance in the giant theater was on that night's schedule, since he never knew what he was destined to experience each night.

On top of this, his father said that Jeremy had been talking in his sleep. This created a new concern for Jeremy. He was troubled that he might unwittingly say something inappropriate. What if he talked about Mr. Daymo in his sleep and his parents heard him? If they learned of the existence of The Secret Club, would they have to be "taken care of," like the hospital nurse with brown eyes who had stolen Jeremy's heart? Although he had no idea what actually happened to the hospital nurse, he was confident it was something very unpleasant.

Because he was on vacation, his parents let his typical bedtime come and go, but they made him turn-in once the nightly news came on at 10:00. As Jeremy nervously lied in bed, he felt his forehead get a little damp and he wiped the cool sweat off with the sleeve of his pajama.

Thankfully, the dreams over the next couple of nights were

much less intense. While talking casually in the front yard of Jeremy's house, Mr. Daymo asked Jeremy whether he thought he could fly. Jeremy was sure that, just like Batman, he didn't have any such superpower.

"I'll bet you could if you really put your mind to it," Mr. Daymo said. When Jeremy looked unconvinced, he added, "Especially if you really *needed* to."

The ground shuddered and deep fissures opened up in the lawn. Mr. Daymo stamped his foot and soared into the air, just as the ground on which he was standing disintegrated and fell into a chasm. Jeremy was poised on a small island of ground. All around him, the yard was breaking up and falling into a deep canyon.

Hovering just above Jeremy, Mr. Daymo encouraged him. "Come on, you can do it. You don't have much time left. It's going to crumble and you'll fall. Come on up and take a gander at the view."

Jeremy held his arms out to keep his balance on his small perch. "What's a gander?"

"It's a kind of goose. Come on, or you'll fall all the way to China."

Jeremy closed his eyes and thought of a goose soaring through the air. He stamped his foot like he had seen Mr. Daymo do, and was surprised when he launched up from the crumbling ground. He hovered in the air beside Mr. Daymo, watching the remainder of his front yard fall into the pit. Jeremy was a little scared of heights and he felt an unpleasant shiver as he stared down at the bottomless chasm. Wanting to get further away from the deep hole, he pumped his right leg and soared higher so that he was floating just above the roof of his house.

From this vantage point, he could see a baseball that was nestled in the gutter and he decided to retrieve it. Jeremy only had partial control over his flight path and he bumped into a tree as he swooped around his house. Several dinosaurs were grazing on his father's lawn, and Jeremy wondered if one of them could help him get the baseball. As if on cue, a dinosaur with a very long neck grabbed the baseball with his mouth and threw it over his shoulder. Jeremy laughed as another dinosaur caught the ball.

Mr. Daymo had grown large white wings and was wearing the costume of the comic book hero Hawkman. "It's amazing what a little terror can do for us, eh Jeremy? It can force us to do things that we never thought possible."

Jeremy enjoyed a few more minutes of flying around his house, and then he suddenly started to plummet back to earth. He waved his arms as if he was flapping wings, but this didn't slow down the free fall. Just before he hit the ground, he woke up in his bed. He had kicked off all of his blankets and the sheet and they were strewn around his bed and on the floor. As he tried to go back to sleep, he thought about the dream. All in all, Jeremy thought that it was an okay dream, despite the ground crumbling under his feet and the sudden loss of his ability to fly.

After late December turned into January, however, these *okay* dreams were the exception, not the rule.

CHAPTER SEVEN

Dr. Glover

In January, Jeremy's parents became increasingly concerned that he was having a scream-inducing nightmare at least four times a week. On those nights when the small house's quiet tranquility was shattered by Jeremy's screams, one or both of his parents rushed into his room. They did their best to calm Jeremy, explaining that bad dreams were just make-believe and that his imagination was causing the nightmares to just *seem* like they were real.

If Jeremy had been asked to list his fears, he would have reported such things as snakes, crocodiles, heights, and skeletons. Every one of these fears made multiple appearances in Jeremy's dreams that month. He had been trapped by snakes and cobras which had appeared out of nowhere in places where you wouldn't expect a serpent to be. Like the one that sprung out of a cookie jar after Jeremy lifted the lid. The crocodiles that terrorized Jeremy were able to attack in both the water and on land. Just as he had seen once on Mutual of Omaha's Wild Kingdom, the crocodiles in Jeremy's dreams moved swiftly on land and were able to drag their prey into and under the murky water that they inhabited. One night, Jeremy felt a crocodile's mouth clamp onto his leg and slowly pull him towards the water before he awoke drenched in sweat.

Jeremy fell from buildings, hot air balloons, and castle towers. As he fell, Jeremy concentrated hard and tried to fly but nothing happened. Every time he fell in a dream, he woke up right before he hit the ground. Skeletons that glowed in the dark chased Jeremy down dark hallways. He could hear the clicking of their bones as they tried to catch him. Regardless of the type of peril he faced, the only thing that saved Jeremy from severe injury or death was waking up.

The increasing severity of his nightmares caused stress on the small Bracken family. Over the course of just a few months, his parents watched Jeremy go from a sound sleeper, to talking in his sleep and finally to having nightmares that caused him to cry out in terror. By the end of January, Jeremy's parents could see a physical toll that the frequent nightmares were having on their son. His overall energy level decreased, and he was no longer a typical rambunctious little boy who was nearly nine years old. Although he still went outside and played with his friends, he did so less often and with less enthusiasm.

While stroking his hands lovingly one night after he had a nightmare, his mother was concerned to see that the cuticle and skin around his fingernails was very dry. She saw dried blood where the delicate skin around his fingernails had cracked open. She asked him if he had been chewing on his fingernails or on his fingertips but Jeremy told her that he had simply scraped his fingers while building a tree fort. Although this was a plausible explanation, Mrs. Bracken didn't believe that it was the truth.

His father's co-workers and his mother's friends noticed that they had dark circles forming under their eyes. Like Jeremy, their faces showed the physical toll that the nightmares were causing. Jeremy was their first and only child and his parents sought advice regarding their son's frequent nightmares from their friends and relatives. The most common piece of advice they received was to make sure that their son didn't eat anything fatty, spicy or rich within a few hours of bedtime. Other than diet advice, almost everyone told them that this "was just a phase" and that just as sudden as the nightmares had come about, they would eventually disappear in time. It seemed that everyone knew of a child who had experienced problems with horrible dreams, and every one of the kids had simply "grown out of it".

Despite these reassurances, Mrs. Bracken was not convinced that her son was just going through a typical cycle of childhood development. On those nights when she ran to his bedroom, his shrieks were often blood-curdling. When she turned on his bedroom light, she saw the abject terror in his eyes. She sometimes had a visceral reaction when she cradled her frightened son in her arms, as if her stomach was being tied into knots. At other times, he was crying before she could reach his bedroom. There was something in those sobs that made her heart hurt as much as her stomach.

On top of all of this, she thought it was curious that Jeremy insisted that he could not remember *anything* about these troubling dreams. On those seldom occasions that she had nightmares, Becky Bracken awoke being able to remember at least generally what horrible thing had occurred in her sleep. There was never a time that she woke up in a cold sweat but couldn't remember *anything* about her troubled dream. As time went on, she became increasingly convinced that her son wasn't telling his parents everything he remembered about his frequent nightmares. At the end of January, his parents concluded that this situation had reached the point that medical intervention was needed.

His mother made an appointment for her son to see their family's doctor. Dr. Glover was a general practitioner who had delivered Jeremy and provided all of his medical needs during his short life, except while he was in the hospital for bowel surgery. While Jeremy was at school, she called and spoke at length with Dr. Glover's nurse, explaining the concerns that she and her husband had regarding Jeremy's frequent nightmares. Mrs. Bracken didn't want to alarm her son, so she told him that he needed to see Dr. Glover just to make sure that he was still recovering fine from November's abdominal surgery.

The night before the office visit, Jeremy dreamt that he was cooking something while standing in their kitchen wearing his mother's apron. Although there was a steaming pot on each of the four burners, he didn't know what he was cooking. Jeremy was barely tall enough to see into the pots. He stood on his tiptoes and saw that each of the pots contained boiling water. Bobbing up and down in the bubbling water were several fiery red whole tomatoes. He looked around to see what other ingredients he had, but all he saw was a small mound of tomatoes on the counter. Jeremy looked at the collection of pots, still unsure as to what he was supposed to be making. Just then, Shaggy and Scooby Doo ran into the kitchen.

"Let's go!" Shaggy urged, as he and Scooby ran through the kitchen and out the back door. Just as Jeremy was about to take Shaggy's advice and run, a cripplingly severe pain seared through his stomach and groin. His body folded in half and he fell to the floor. Just as his knees struck the linoleum, the kitchen floor turned into water, and Jeremy was floating in a large above-ground swimming pool. When the pain in his belly let up, Jeremy saw Mr. Daymo standing in the pool's waist-high water in his dark suit.

"Big day tomorrow," Mr. Daymo said.

Jeremy didn't know what Mr. Daymo was talking about. "What big day?" Suddenly, Jeremy became convinced that he was supposed to visit the circus the next day. "Yeah, I hope I see elephants!" Jeremy replied in an excited voice.

Mr. Daymo rubbed the area between his eyes with his thumb and forefinger. He shook his head and said, "Not a circus. You are seeing Dr. Glover tomorrow!"

"That's right, I am," Jeremy replied. He shook his head and asked, "Why did I think that I was going to the circus?"

"Never mind that. Here's what you need to know. Mum's the word when it comes to what you tell the doctor tomorrow."

"What's mum's?"

"It's a colorful flower. You say *nothing* to the doctor, got it?" Jeremy nodded his head slowly and unconvincingly. "Kid, remember that you are in The Secret Club. No one can know about us, otherwise *very* bad things happen." Mr. Daymo looked so intensely at Jeremy that he thought that the man's eyes were going to burn a hole in Jeremy's head.

Cautiously, Jeremy said, "Like what happened to the nurse?"

"That's my boy!" he went to slap his thigh but since it was underwater, he instead just made the "ok" hand gesture.

"By the way, what *did* happen to the nurse? You never told me."

Mr. Daymo's mouth was moving but he wasn't making any sound. Instead of hearing Mr. Daymo's voice, Jeremy only heard the infectious refrain from *Bad Blood*, a song that had been playing a lot on the radio. It was a duet sung by Elton John and Neal Sedaker, or something like that. The title of the song was repeated over and over again by the two singers. "Baaad, baaad, blood, blood."

Mr. Daymo lit a cigarette. Sitting on the edge of the pool behind Mr. Daymo, Jeremy saw a lit candle in the shape of a woman. The candle was melting very quickly. "Was *that* the nurse who was melting?" Jeremy thought to himself and this was what he was thinking when he awoke.

Jeremy wasn't afraid of the doctor's office. Despite the fact that he was usually seeing Dr. Glover because something bad had happened to him, Jeremy thought that the old doctor was a pretty cool guy. He wasn't as cool as James Bond, but who was? He was always friendly and sometimes told a funny joke during the office visit.

When the nurse called Jeremy's name, his mother asked him to sit tight. She told Jeremy that she was going to talk to Dr. Glover for a couple of minutes while Jeremy remained in the waiting room. While his mother was gone, Jeremy unenthusiastically flipped through the copy of *Highlights* magazine, but there was nothing of particular interest in it. The nurse called Jeremy's name again, and he followed her to an examination room where his mother and Dr. Glover were waiting.

"What's all this I hear about you becoming the next big football star?" Dr. Glover asked with his trademark warm smile.

"No, I don't think I'm very good," Jeremy replied shyly as he blushed.

"Well, young man, let's get you up here and give you the once over," the doctor said cheerfully, patting the exam table.

Dr. Glover took his time examining Jeremy, pressing and poking all over his body. Throughout the examination, Dr. Glover made small talk with his young patient so that Jeremy's attention was engaged and he was less likely to become apprehensive. Mrs. Bracken stood in the corner of the room, biting her thumbnail nervously. After he looked in his eyes, ears and throat, Dr. Glover asked Jeremy to unbuckle his pants so that he could see the surgical scar and examine his lower abdomen. From several different angles, the doctor slowly pushed his fingers deep into Jeremy's abdomen, asking him if this caused any pain. One time there was a little tenderness but all of the other times Dr. Glover pressed into his abdomen, it felt fine. Dr. Glover asked him questions about his abdomen such as how often it hurt, whether he had pain when he pooped, and stuff like that. Jeremy was truthful and told Dr. Glover that at times he would have episodes of sharp, burning pain but it typically only lasted a short time.

"Is there something that seems to bring on the pain? Like a certain kind of food or if you do a certain activity?" his doctor asked.

Jeremy felt a little spasm in his abdomen. It wasn't a searing, hot poker type pain nor was it one of his painful cramps; just a little tickle in his belly. "Nope. Not that I can think of," he replied. Jeremy of course wasn't going to tell the doctor that these sharp pains signaled that a man by the name of Mr. Daymo was near.

When Dr. Glover abruptly changed the subject, Jeremy was taken off guard. "How've you been sleeping lately, Jeremy?" The small tickle in his belly became an uncomfortable spasm when the doctor asked him this question.

Jeremy looked down to buckle his belt so that he could momentarily hide his face, in case the spasm had caused him to wince a little. "Pretty good," Jeremy said, trying to sound upbeat and carefree. He managed to chuckle a little and added, "Mom and Dad say I talk in my sleep."

Dr. Glover had kind eyes, but Jeremy nevertheless could feel them burrowing into him. Jeremy looked up and met the old doctor's eyes. Jeremy recognized at that moment that Dr. Glover was a funny and likable fellow but he was also very sharp and perceptive.

"When you have a really bad dream, what do you dream about?"

"I don't know," Jeremy responded. Dr. Glover continued to look at Jeremy, and the boy decided that this answer was not going to be adequate. "I just know that it was something bad, like a monster or something chasing me."

"How do you feel when you wake up?" the doctor asked in a very nonchalant tone of voice.

"Okay. Sometimes I'm still a little tired, but Mom says I have to go to school even if I'm tired." Once again, Jeremy tried to sound breezy, but his words sounded to him to be strained and fake. He looked over to his mother and she flashed a nervous smile.

Dr. Glover chuckled, saying, "And she is one hundred percent right!" The doctor slapped his hand on his thigh to punctuate his statement and Jeremy's eyes got big.

The only person he'd ever seen slap his thigh like that was Mr. Daymo. A charge of lightning ran down Jeremy's spine and he was suddenly concerned that he might be in a dream. Was Dr. Glover actually Dr. Daymo? Jeremy scrutinized the doctor, trying to detect any change in his face that would reveal that it was actually Dr. Daymo who'd performed the physical examination. Before he got a good look at the doctor's face, he turned his back on Jeremy and asked his mother to step out of the room with him for a moment.

As they walked out of the exam room, Jeremy watched them carefully, trying to detect anything that was out of place. Once they closed the door, he made a quick inventory of what he saw in the small exam room. Everything looked normal and nothing appeared to be out of place. The glass jars sitting on the shelf were filled with cotton balls, Q-tips, and gauze, as opposed to something out-of-place like bow ties, butterflies, or spiders. Or little tomatoes. The growth chart on the wall, the blood pressure machine and the sad hobo clown picture on the wall all looked just as they did during the many times Jeremy had been in Dr. Glover's little exam room. While it was often difficult to know for sure that you were in a dream, Jeremy was eventually convinced that this visit to Dr. Glover was *not* a dream: he was in the real world. He took a deep breath and gave a sigh of relief.

Jeremy relaxed a little and absently looked at the painting of the sad hobo clown on the wall. When he shifted his weight, the white paper covering the examination table crackled. Jeremy's mind wandered. What did Dr. Glover do with all of the leftover paper from the exam tables? Was it ironed and then re-used? Did he send it to a factory somewhere to be chopped up into confetti?

As Jeremy continued to wait, he thought of how odd it was that Dr. Glover asked him about his sleep. How well someone was sleeping didn't seem like a subject that a doctor would get into with his patients. You might talk to a gypsy with a crystal ball about sleeping and what kind of dreams you had so she could tell your fortune, but Jeremy couldn't think of any reason why someone would need to talk to their doctor about dreams.

Since Dr. Glover had asked him about his sleep and his dreams, Jeremy concluded that the doctor must have some additional knowledge on the subject. This caused Jeremy to contemplate how far Dr. Glover's skills in this area reached. Were doctors trained to peer into their patient's dreams? Was it possible that the doctor somehow had an uncanny ability to see into Jeremy's dreams? If that was true, did the doctor know of Mr. Daymo? The Secret Club? No, that was silly, he told himself. He concluded that Dr. Glover was just curious and asked him about his dreams simply as a matter of polite conversation. Jeremy was satisfied with this conclusion, and he never considered the possibility that his mother had told the old doctor about her son's frequent nightmares.

Above the sink was a tall white cabinet with glass doors. In the cabinet were medical devices, a few small boxes marked "SANITIZED," and a couple small glass containers. Jeremy knew from firsthand experience that the little glass bottles held medicine that was sucked up into syringes. He shuddered a little when he thought about getting shots. Jeremy's young mind wondered how many different drugs there were in the world. As his mind wandered, Jeremy suddenly had an *"ah-ha!"* moment. He wondered if Dr. Glover had access to a medicine that could help Jeremy control his dreams. As soon as Jeremy had this thought, he experienced a twinge of pain in the area below and to the right of his belly button.

Dr. Glover came back into the room alone. He had a big smile on his face, just as Jeremy had seen many times. "Well, young man, it looks like things are going well. You're healing up just like the surgeon and I hoped you would. You're not too old for a Tootsie Roll, are you?" Jeremy shook his head eagerly and the doctor reached into his white coat pocket, pulling out a junior size Tootsie Roll. As he handed the candy to Jeremy, Dr. Glover said, "Do me a favor, Jeremy, and let your folks know if you start having any problems trying go to the toilet, okay?" Jeremy nodded as he unwrapped the piece of chocolate. "If the pain you have in your stomach and down by your belly button starts getting worse or the pain happens more often, I need you to promise me that you'll tell your parents. Will you promise to do that?"

"Okay, I promise."

"Since you made that promise, I think it calls for another Tootsie Roll for Mr. Jeremy!" After he handed over another piece of candy, the doctor tucked the young patient's file under his arm and held out his right hand. "Good to see you, my young friend. Have a very good spring and try not to break too many hearts!"

Jeremy's hand was swallowed up in the doctor's hand and Jeremy replied truthfully, "Thanks, but I never want to break *anyone's* heart." The doctor laughed and Jeremy slid off the exam table. Just as Dr. Glover was about to pull open the examination room door, Jeremy decided to ask a question. With a mouth that had partially chewed chocolate in it, Jeremy asked, "Dr. Glover? Is there such a thing as a medicine that can stop nightmares?" As soon as the words had come out of his mouth, a big, painful spasm hit his guts. He gritted his teeth when the pain hit. Jeremy hoped that the doctor wouldn't see the muscles in his face tense. If he did, Jeremy hoped that the doctor would conclude that he was simply chewing the Tootsie Roll.

Dr. Glover kept his hand on the handle but didn't open the door. He turned to Jeremy and looked over the top of his bifocals. "Why do you ask that? Are you having a lot of nightmares?"

The way that Dr. Glover was looking at him made Jeremy feel very uneasy. Jeremy had the sensation that he'd walked up to the edge of a cliff and was looking down. "Just a few," Jeremy lied. Between the doctor's look and the sudden pain in his abdomen, Jeremy quickly concluded that asking the question was a mistake and that he needed to end this conversation right away. "Someone at school said that there was a pill that did that but I told them they were full of it!" He did his best to smile, even though he could feel his guts spasm.

Dr. Glover continued to look at Jeremy intently and then smiled. "Not that I know of, young man. Just think pleasant thoughts as you are going to sleep: that's the best remedy to keep bad dreams away."

Dr. Glover opened the door and they left the room. His mother was waiting for him and she once again smiled in a way that looked as though it took a great deal of effort for her to do so. On the ride home, Jeremy thought that he may have initially overestimated the doctor's level of knowledge and training as it relates to sleeping and dreaming. If the best remedy he could come up was "think happy thoughts", then maybe the doctor wasn't as smart as Jeremy had first thought.

The night of his visit with Dr. Glover, Jeremy dreamt that he was sitting on a very tall chair that had legs about six feet long. Under the long legged chair, the ground undulated as thousands of snakes swirled around the chair. Jeremy quickly pulled his legs to his body and tucked his knees under his chin as he watched the snakes crawling over each other. There were so many snakes that they looked like a body of water. The ground was an ocean of slithering serpents, lapping up against the chair legs. He tried his best not to move at all, but the chair was already starting to sway on its long, thin rickety legs. At times, snakes bumped into one of the chair legs, and Jeremy swayed precariously in the opposite direction in order to stabilize the weight on the chair. Jeremy looked around for something that he could jump onto or grab but there was nothing.

A large boa constrictor firmly wrapped around one of the fragile chair's back legs, and Jeremy felt the chair start to tip forward. He pushed himself to the back of the chair, trying to shift his weight in the opposite direction. As he did so, it felt like a searing hot poker had been stuck into his bowels, and Jeremy cried out in pain. The sudden intense pain caused Jeremy to lurch forward and this was enough to cause the unstable chair to tip over. As Jeremy was about to plunge into the ocean of snakes, the dream ended abruptly. Instead of swimming in a swirling whirlpool of snakes, he was back in his bed. Once he realized where he was, Jeremy looked down anxiously and was thankful to see that there were no snakes writhing on the floor. Jeremy took a deep breath and sighed in relief.

"Are you okay, honey?" he heard his mother ask from the hallway.

"Yes, mom" Jeremy replied a little breathlessly. His pajama shirt was stuck to his chest because he was sweating.

From the hallway, she asked, "Do you want a drink of water?" Before Jeremy could answer, she flipped on the bedroom light and added, "How about a tomato?"

As soon as his mother asked this question, another sudden and intense pain shot through his belly. Jeremy saw that it was Mr. Daymo who walked into the bedroom, wearing his mother's housecoat and slippers. When Mr. Daymo's mouth moved, his mom's voice came out of it. "I'm a little disappointed with your little gesture at Dr. Glover's office," Mother Daymo chided. "But, I guess it's the bailiwick of headstrong young boys to push their boundaries."

The pain in his belly prevented Jeremy from responding but he thought to himself, "A bailiwick?"

"It's a jurisdictional designation," Mother Daymo said, standing in the middle of the room and putting her hands on her hips. "I guess the best way for the livestock to learn the boundaries of the pasture is for them to bump into the electric fence from time to time. You know, *bzzzzz!*" Mother Daymo reached inside the housecoat and pulled out a large tomato. "This visit to Dr. Glover shows us that you are falling down on the job, young man. You need to do a better job of acting like a regular rug rat. If you continue to be a downer, your parents are going to think that there's something really wrong with you," Mother Daymo explained, tossing the tomato up into the air and catching it in the same hand like it was a baseball.

"If they think something is wrong, then they might get more professional assistance. It's in those circumstances when young boys can make mistakes, do you understand what I'm saying?" Some of the pain had gone away, but Jeremy was still lying on the bed and in no shape to give a verbal reply.

"Mistakes lead to bad things happening, don't they?" Mother Daymo's head suddenly ignited and was swallowed in flames like she was a match. The flame quickly moved down her body and she melted, leaving nothing but the housecoat and the tomato sitting on Jeremy's bedroom floor.

Jeremy cried out in horror and sat up in bed. He heard someone running towards his room and he braced himself for what was about to enter his bedroom. His mother whipped open the door and scurried to his bedside. Without saying a word, she pulled Jeremy to her and hugged him. Initially, Jeremy was stiff, but when his mother squeezed him, he relaxed in her loving embrace.

"It's just a dream," his mother repeated over and over again. He glanced over her shoulder and saw that the housecoat and tomato were no longer on the bedroom floor. She sat on his bed and put his head on her shoulder, rocking him back and forth as she said, "Doctor says these nightmares will go away in time. Shhhhhhh."

The next day, Jeremy thought a lot about the dream with the chair, the snakes and the incendiary Mother Daymo in it. It was after the dreams where he believed he was in danger of being injured or killed that Jeremy's imagination ran wild. The following day after such nightmares, all he could do was to think about what *could* have happened to him. Would he have been bitten if he fell into the ocean of snakes? Would he be killed? He didn't know what happened when you died in a dream, and he had no interest in finding out. Some of the kids at school said that if you died in your dream, you died in real life. Jeremy's initial thought was that this was absurd. If this was true, then he would have heard of stories of people who were found in bed without a head because it had been torn off by a monster that was stalking them in their dream. If people were truly discovering the mangled bodies of loved ones who had been fatally run over by giant steamrollers in their sleep, Jeremy figured that he would have heard something about such events.

After he thought the whole thing through, he felt pretty confident that death in a dream did not automatically result in real life death. A little bit later, however, he wondered if you just wouldn't wake up if you died in your sleep. If you were a victim of a beheading in your dream, maybe your body looked fine but you just never woke up. There was no doubt that there was a danger of dying in a dream, especially if you had the vivid dreams like Jeremy had. After he thought about it for most of the day, Jeremy was still not sure what happened if you died while you were in a dream.

When he was walking home from school, he remembered something that Dr. Glover said about keeping away nightmares. The old doctor said that the best remedy was to think happy thoughts. Jeremy decided that this was a real medical strategy and not just an adult's idle words said in passing to a child. Jeremy thought back to his mood before the nightmares began in November. When the nightly dreams had begun, Jeremy considered himself a pretty happy boy. He had his own bedroom. He got a new bike the previous Christmas and his parents were okay, as parents go. However, as the nightly visitations continued to invade his sleep, he felt that his energy was very slowly being sucked away.

He was aware that he spent more and more of his waking

hours thinking about the previous night's dream and worrying about what was going to happen in his dream later that night. Maybe, Jeremy thought, he was in a vicious loop: the more dreams he had, the more tired and rundown he became, and as a result, more nightmares came. If he could somehow break this vicious cycle, maybe the encounters with the man in the dark suit would diminish. Or end altogether.

After he got home and changed clothes, Jeremy called his best friend Rob and suggested they go to the gas station on the other side of the neighborhood to buy comic books. When it came to turning a regular school day into a happy day, Jeremy concluded that the most effective tools were his best friend Rob, comic books, and Bazooka bubble gum. Jeremy took 30 cents out of the hidden stash of coins he kept in a Mason jar in his closet. The February air was brisk but neither of the boys paid much attention. They were too busy talking and laughing as they made their way to the gas station to worry about their cold ears or red noses.

As they walked, they discussed several different subjects that were of great importance to them. These included such topics as their teacher (why she was so mean and whether they could prove definitively that she was indeed a witch); who would win in a fight between Batman and Joe Frazier (the Dark Knight); what the best kind of pop was (Jeremy argued it was Coca-Cola, but Rob insisted that Vess Root Beer was the best); if anyone could possibly beat the Harlem Globetrotters (no way).

At the gas station, Jeremy bought a *Justice League of America* comic book and two pieces of bubble gum with his 30 cents. Rob's favorite comic (*Spider-Man*) was sold out, so he settled for a *Captain America* and a couple of Pixie Stix. While lounging on a picnic table in the park, they read their comic books. Jeremy gave Rob one of his pieces of Bazooka and they read the gum's cartoon inserts to each other. They took a different route to get home and followed a small creek. There was a shallow portion that had frozen over, and the boys used rocks to break up the ice. It was a very, very satisfying afternoon.

During supper, Jeremy was upbeat and talkative. His mother inquired, "Did you and Rob have a big ballyhoo?"

"A bailey-what?" Jeremy asked.

"You've never heard of a ballyhoo?" his mother asked, scooping out another helping of tuna casserole onto Jeremy's plate. "A ballyhoo is a fish."

"Oh, okay," Jeremy said, scrunching his eyebrows together. He wasn't sure that he understood how the word was being used, but he was in much too good of a mood to get bogged down in a conversation with his mother about semantics. "I guess we did. Yeah."

There wasn't any homework that he needed to do that night, so Jeremy was allowed to watch some television with his parents. They watched a variety show that included some boring old people singing. Slowly, Jeremy felt his good mood diminish as the awful singers sang an equally awful song. Fortunately, there were a couple funny skits in the show, so Jeremy was able to keep his good mood afloat. While he was brushing his teeth and getting ready for bed, Jeremy was optimistic that his efforts to keep happy thoughts in his head would pay off that night.

He fell asleep thinking about that day's satisfying consumption of sugary bubble gum and comic books. Jeremy found himself standing in a small clearing that was surrounded by dense woods. He looked around and all he could see were pine trees. The trees extended out from the small clearing; Jeremy couldn't see where they ended. It was as if he had parachuted into the only clearing in the middle of a huge, dense forest.

Before he could come up with a reason as to why he was in the forest, the trees started to ignite. One by one, all of the trees that encircled the clearing suddenly caught on fire, trapping Jeremy.

He felt the heat radiating from the conflagration and he coughed when he breathed some of the thick smoke. He was trapped, and he was going to be cooked like a hot dog thrown into a campfire.

The sudden abdominal pain that Jeremy had experienced so many times before hit him once again and he dropped to one knee as he moaned. Through the gray smoke, Jeremy thought he could see someone or something approaching the clearing from the thicket of pine trees. It looked like it was walking through the heart of the fire. As quickly as the fire started, it went out.

Jeremy remained on one knee, amazed that he was now surrounded by hundreds of smoldering trees. The smoke cascading from the burnt trees was thick and black. Out of the smoke emerged Smokey the Bear, holding a metal bucket in his left paw. The bear's face had been replaced by Mr. Daymo's. Smokey the Daymo looked tired and he walked with a bit of a limp. Without looking at Jeremy or speaking, the bear dumped his pail of water onto one of the smoldering trees. The tree hissed when the water struck it.

Smokey the Daymo turned and began to trudge back into the smoking forest. After a few steps, the bear turned towards Jeremy and said in Mr. Daymo's distinctive voice, "Sometimes it's the dark water that extinguishes the flames." He then turned back and disappeared into the smoke. Jeremy was too scared to leave the clearing; eventually, he was swallowed up in dark smoke.

The next day, Jeremy made another effort to think happy thoughts to chase away his dreams. It didn't work. He dreamt that he was being dive bombed by odd looking birds that pecked menacingly at his head. It was clear that thinking happy was not a cure to his nightmares. Dr. Glover's suggested cure was apparently of no value. Jeremy had high hopes for the medical cure and when it failed, he was very disappointed. He wondered if there was *anything* that could be done to break the cycle of dreams.

His sour mood was quickly swept away when his parents informed him during supper that they were going to visit his grandparents the following weekend. As Jeremy thought excitedly about seeing his grandparents, an interesting question came to mind. If he was at the most wonderful place on the planet, would it keep away the nightmares?

CHAPTER EIGHT

Grandma & Grandpa's House

The following Friday, the family packed up for an overnight visit to see his grandparents, who lived on the other side of the state. When they arrived, Jeremy's grandmother gave him a big hug and squeezed him so hard it took his breath away. Grandpa stood next to Jeremy and compared their heights. "You must be part weed, you're growing so fast!" his grandpa proclaimed.

While the grown-ups talked, Jeremy went outside and played with his grandparents' dog, Smokey. Jeremy and the dog ran around the yard, and Smokey retrieved tennis balls that Jeremy threw. Jeremy didn't have a dog at home because his dad had allergies, so he looked forward to spending time with Smokey. A few hours later, Grandma called everyone to the kitchen to enjoy the feast she had spent many hours preparing. Jeremy understood that his mother learned all of her cooking skills from Grandma. However, something went haywire during the learning process, because his grandma's cooking was way better than his mom's.

Jeremy couldn't stop eating because everything Grandma made tasted so good. As always, Grandma's roast beef was salty and fell apart when a fork was put into it. The green beans were buttery and just as crisp as potato chips. Jeremy thought he'd never been as full as he was when he walked away from the table that night. For the rest of the evening, the huge meal made Jeremy feel lethargic but satisfied. He even went to bed before his parents told him to do so because he was so tired.

He slept in one of the extra bedrooms by himself. It was an old and drafty house, so he bundled himself in the quilts that Grandma had laid out at the foot of the bed. Very quickly, he faded off into sleep and didn't wake up until mid-morning. He awoke refreshed for the first time in months. Jeremy had a vague recollection of having a short dream about a dog but that was it. There had been no visit from Mr. Daymo. Instead of waking up with all kinds of odd images racing through his head, that morning he felt unburdened and free. His brain felt like it had been reset and was eagerly ready for the day to begin. It had been so long since he felt this way, Jeremy had almost forgotten what it was like. There was a big happy smile on his face when he ate his late breakfast.

The five of them went shopping and had supper that night at a fancy restaurant where you had to keep a cloth white napkin in your lap as you ate. That night, Jeremy once again slept soundly and was not plagued by bizarre dreams or frightening nightmares. Jeremy thought about Dr. Glover's cure once again. He wondered if the happiness of spending time with his grandparents had successfully chased away the dreams. When he woke up on the second morning, he was as happy as if it was his birthday. The entire family slept soundly for two nights and felt the best that they had in weeks. During the drive back home, his dad turned up the radio, and the three of them sang along to the music.

By the time they got home on Sunday night, the Bracken trio was tired and ready to turn in. When he went to sleep that night, Jeremy wasn't thinking at all about Mr. Daymo. He was so exhausted he hadn't considered whether the dreams would return now that he was back in his own bed. Jeremy was very tired, and he thought about very little before he fell asleep. Jeremy was pleasantly surprised when slept through the night and once again woke up feeling refreshed. There were no dreams that he needed to relive or analyze the next day. Three nights in a row of dreamless sleep: it was great!

When he got out of bed and stood up, though, he felt as if the house was gently moving from side to side. He staggered a little as he made his way across the room and looked out his bedroom window. Instead of looking out over their backyard, all Jeremy could see was water. It appeared as if the house was bobbing up and down the waves of an ocean. Trying to keep his balance, Jeremy walked unsteadily to his bedroom door. When he opened it, he discovered that the hallway was gone. Instead of being in his house, he found that he was on the deck of an old wooden sailing ship. Sailors dressed in white uniforms were scurrying around the ship, adjusting the sails and barking out orders.

"Now I remember," Jeremy thought to himself. "I live on a ship. Why did I think I lived in a house? I live on a ship that sails around the world." How could he have forgotten this important fact? For as long as he could remember, he'd lived on this ship as it sailed the high seas. He tried to remember if he had a job on the ship but came up with nothing. As he stood on the deck of the ship in his pajamas and looked around, he concluded that he apparently didn't live on a pirate ship, as the ship's well-dressed crew didn't look like shabby pirates. This still left a number of nagging questions running through his mind. What kind of ship was this and who owned it? Did he still go to school on the ship, or had he given that up?

From behind him, a happy voice said, "Good morning! Today's gonna be grrreat!" Jeremy turned around and saw Tony the Tiger from the Frosted Flakes commercials. The large tiger stood upright on his back legs and sported a white sailor's hat between his upturned orange ears. Tony started gyrating his hips and waving his arms in an impromptu hula dance. The other sailors stopped what they were doing and began to dance as well. Everyone on the deck of the ship (except for Jeremy) was doing the hula. They did so without any musical accompaniment, and they seemed to be enjoying themselves.

"What am I supposed to be doing on this ship?" Jeremy asked Tony the Tiger. "Where are we?"

Without stopping his hula dance, Tony replied, "We're sailing the seven seas. Everyone knows that!"

"Okay, but what am *I* supposed to be doing? Am I the captain? The cook?"

Tony stopped dancing. All the sailors stopped as well. "You're supposed to be learning everything you can so that you'll be ready," Tony responded seriously. Jeremy felt a familiar wrenching sensation in his gut, and he watched Tony the Tiger's face morph so that Mr. Daymo's eyes were now looking at Jeremy. "Remember? The whole, 'You are the chosen one' kind of thing?" Daymo the Tiger said. A large leather bound book appeared in the tiger's large paws, and he handed it to Jeremy. "Here. This will help you. Think of it as a basic user's manual for the job. Read it carefully. Get everything you can out of this tome."

"Tome?" Jeremy asked.

"It's a cutting instrument," Daymo the Tiger responded. "Pore over it. Really get into the book. Absorb it." The tiger tittered a little under his breath as Jeremy took the book from him. It was thick and very heavy. Just by looking at the weathered and stained leather cover, Jeremy could tell that it was very old. "Go ahead, it's yours to keep," Daymo the Tiger said in a very enthusiastic voice. "Honest. I want you to be ready for the halcyon days that are coming for you very soon!"

"Hal...."

"Halcyon. It's a bird. Go ahead and squeeze it to your chest. No one can ever take the knowledge in that book away from you, Jeremy!"

Jeremy hesitatingly brought the book to his chest while Daymo the Tiger nodded his head with approval. When the book touched his chest, it began to sink into his body. It was if his chest was quicksand and the book was being sucked into Jeremy's body. Jeremy managed to get a grip on the edge of the cover and he tried to pull it out of his body, but the book's descent into his chest cavity was unstoppable. As the book entered his body, Jeremy heard a high pitched whine in his ears. He swatted at his ears because it sounded like a swarm of noisy mosquitoes were in them. After a few moments, the sound became a little clearer, and he heard what sounded like a thousand voices whispering in his ears. It was if a multitude of people were all whispering a secret to Jeremy at the same time. In this avalanche of mish-mashed voices, Jeremy was unable to make out any specific words. He looked down at his chest and the book was gone. As the whispering continued, Jeremy felt as though there was something crawling in his ears. It started out as a tickling sensation and then grew to be an unpleasant pulsing pressure.

Jeremy rubbed his ears vigorously, but they continued to itch and the pressure inside continued to increase. The voices became more high-pitched, and it felt like the chorus of voices had gnawed through his ears and were now burrowing their way into his brain. Jeremy used his fists to pound his ears, trying to dislodge the invaders. Another sudden jolt of pain deep in his ear canals caused him to fall to his knees. Jeremy thought a pencil had been pushed all the way through his ears and into his brain.

From his kneeling position, he put his forehead on the ships' rough wood deck. When he closed his eyes, he saw images flash in front of him, as if someone was spinning the knob of a filmstrip projector as fast as they could. The pressure in his ears intensified and his entire head began to throb with a dull aching pain. Jeremy started banging his forehead on the deck of the ship. When he awoke, he was banging his head on the hardwood floor of his bedroom. His mother and father rushed into the room and knelt beside him. His father put his hand on the floor so that Jeremy's head hit his open palm instead of the floor. His mother was gently shaking Jeremy's shoulders and repeatedly saying his name. "Jeremy! Jeremy! Wake up, hon."

Jeremy looked first at his mother and then his father, both of whom were gazing at him with fear and concern. Jeremy pulled up his pajama top and looked at his chest but he didn't see anything unusual. There was no apparent wound or scar that the old book left after being absorbed into his body. Jeremy cried tears of bitter disappointment. He had dared to hope that the time with his grandparents had broken the cycle of nightmares and that he was finally free. His heart felt shattered when he realized that he was wrong.

Disappointment is an extremely strong emotion for a child. Dr. Freud and other experts in the field of pediatric psychology have written about why this is so. Adults can seek comfort from their disappointments by calling upon any number of metaphors and proverbs to help them through such events. Old sayings like "there are more fish in the ocean" have been taken to heart by adults and used to successfully blunt the pain of disappointment. In addition, the sheer number of such events that an adult endures during their life builds up scar tissue that helps reduce the sting of disappointment. Kids, on the other hand, haven't developed their protective scar tissue. They usually don't fully understand the adult world's soothing metaphors and as a result, disappointment's bite is harsh. Disappointment was a heavy yoke that Jeremy bore on his small shoulders. He felt as deflated as if summer vacation had been cancelled and replaced with months of spelling tests. The cycle of nightmares hadn't been broken.

After that night, his parents noticed that Jeremy's mood took a definite turn for the worse. Once again, the detached, sullen version of Jeremy returned. The essence of their son was still there, but it was as if he wore a gray veil that muted all of his actions and emotions. His parents once again began discussing whether they should look for a specialist who might be able to help Jeremy.

As Jeremy was staring blankly at his math textbook and the teacher continued to drone on about how to determine a number's lowest common denominator, he thought fondly about the two wonderful nights of sleep he had enjoyed the previous weekend. He reminisced about how refreshed and energetic he felt the previous Saturday and Sunday morning after a dreamless night. If only he could have brought Grandma and Grandpa's bed home with him—the bed that had somehow protected him from Mr. Daymo.

This thread of thought led Jeremy to consider the abilities of Mr. Daymo. Was there a limit on the power that Mr. Daymo had? Could it be that he was powerful while Jeremy was in his bed but a weakling if Jeremy wasn't in his bedroom? Jeremy felt a *zing* of excitement shoot through his body. If Mr. Daymo's powers were somehow tied to Jeremy's bed, any change in the sleeping arrangement could reduce that power. Yes, Mr. Daymo had visited him in his hospital bed in November but that seemed different from what Jeremy was going through now.

With renewed hope, Jeremy considered what he could do to decrease Mr. Daymo's power. Initially, he considered sleeping on a blanket on his bedroom floor. The more he thought about it, however, the more he didn't think this would be much of a hurdle for Mr. Daymo to clear. Jeremy remembered that some of his dreams had caused him to fall to his bedroom's floor, and yet the fiend was still able to control his dreams. Just sleeping on the floor didn't seem like it would slow Dr. Daymo down. He concluded that he needed to escape the confines of his bedroom in order to tax Mr. Daymo's powers. There was an old couch stored in his house's small and musty basement, and Jeremy decided this would be a good place to sleep that night.

He managed to stay awake after being put to bed and waited patiently for his parents to go to sleep later that night. Jeremy read a Hardy Boys book under the bed covers with the aid of a flashlight so he could stay awake. Once he thought his parents were asleep, Jeremy quietly crept down to the basement and curled up on the old sofa. The sofa arm where Jeremy laid his head had a bit of a musty, mildewy smell, but it was soft and Jeremy fell asleep quickly.

Jeremy was a raccoon. He was running around an overgrown pasture and simply enjoying being alive. Jeremy frolicked in the field, darting amongst the trees. Running on all fours felt very natural to him and as far as he could remember, he'd always been able to use his sharp claws to scramble up tree trunks. In the midst of his playing, Jeremy remembered he needed to collect nuts for the upcoming winter.

Jeremy then turned into a fluffy brown squirrel. He found an acorn lying on the ground and picked it up. For some reason, Jeremy couldn't remember where he was supposed to take the nuts. There had to be someplace that he was storing food but despite racking his brain, Jeremy couldn't remember where all of his other nuts were hidden. As he tried to remember, he thought he would take a few nibbles of the acorn in order to get some *brain food*. Where, oh where was he supposed to take the nut? After he took a few small bites of the acorn, Jeremy's squirrel stomach clenched, causing him to drop the acorn to the grass.

"Winter will be here soon," came a voice from beside Jeremy. With his gut still quivering with pain, Jeremy the Squirrel opened one eye and was not the least bit surprised to see a tall black rabbit standing next to him, smoking a cigarette. He had big hind feet and stood upright, like the drawing of Brer Rabbit in Jeremy's old Uncle Remus storybook. "I see you're already storing up for winter. You're planning and thinking ahead. That's smart. Real smart, my boy. You seem to be trying to remember something. Are you looking for your cache of nuts?"

"A what of nuts?" Jeremy asked.

"Cache. It means money." When Brer Daymo exhaled, the smoke that blew towards Jeremy smelled like a combination of bleach and the fabric softener that mother used. "Come on, let's go."

Brer Daymo hopped towards a decrepit old barn but Jeremy the Squirrel decided he didn't want to follow him. He felt strongly that he needed to prepare for winter, not follow a talking rabbit. Picking up his acorn, he sat on his haunches and watched the rabbit hop towards the faded red barn. Without any warning, Jeremy the Squirrel was picked up and flown swiftly all the way to the barn door as if a hurricane strength wind was carrying him. Brer Daymo held the barn door open with one paw and gestured with his other paw. "Beauty before age," he snickered.

The hurricane force wind blew once again, throwing open the door. The gust picked Jeremy up and dumped him into the barn. When the door was slammed behind him, Jeremy let out a surprised *yip*. Blinding white floodlight filled the inside of the barn and as soon as his eyes adjusted to the glare, Jeremy saw that the barn was full of animals. It appeared that no two animals were alike. The menagerie was not limited to just farm animals. There was a giraffe, a tiger, a rhinoceros, and plenty of other animals you would only see in a zoo. All of them were facing Jeremy as if they had been waiting to throw him a big surprise party. At first, the barn was silent as Jeremy surveyed the group of animals, and they stared at Jeremy blankly.

Simultaneously, all of the animals started making noises as if they were all saying "Surprise!" in their native tongue. The rooster crowed, the elephant trumpeted, the lion roared and the mouse squeaked. The barn went from being as quiet as a church to as loud as a rock concert in a blink of an eye. The animals continued speaking loudly to Jeremy and he put his small squirrel paws over his little squirrel ears for relief. Just as suddenly as they had started, the animals became quiet.

In the silence that followed, the animals peeled from the group one by one and ran past Jeremy. Once an animal reached the far wall of the barn, it disappeared in a white puff of smoke. The doe ran past Jeremy. *Poof!* The crocodile lumbered past Jeremy. *Poof!* When the last of the animals had run past Jeremy, Brer Daymo put his paw on Jeremy and said, "Everything and everybody talks to us. We just have to make an effort to listen." The floodlights were turned off, and Jeremy stood in the dark barn. As he stood in the darkness and tried to make sense of what just happened, he heard his father's voice call to him from a distance.

"There you are, little man," Jeremy's dad said. "How come you're downstairs?" Jeremy opened his eyes and saw his father leaning over the couch. "Did you get too hot in your bedroom?" his father asked, putting the back of his hand on Jeremy's forehead. "You don't feel warm." Jeremy was still disoriented and didn't say anything.

Jeremy looked around and saw he was no longer in a barn. As his father was speaking, Jeremy was still trying to figure out where the barn had gone. "Come on, let me take you upstairs," he said, picking up his son and carrying him back to his bedroom. Jeremy just barely woke up during all of this and as soon as his father laid him down on his bed, Jeremy was quickly back to sleep. Thankfully, there were no more dreams that night. Or at least none he could remember the following morning.

As he ate breakfast the next morning, Jeremy was dispirited that sleeping on the sofa had not kept Mr. Daymo away. Although it wasn't a scary nightmare, it was clear that Mr. Daymo's abilities weren't limited to Jeremy's bedroom. The fact that it hadn't been a *scary* dream raised an interesting question, however. Was the dream about the animals a watered-down version of a nightmare? If he had been sleeping in his bed would the animal dream have been more intense and darker? Was there a possibility, Jeremy wondered, that Mr. Daymo's power was reduced when Jeremy wasn't in his bedroom, and this was the reason that he hadn't had a nightmare featuring talking animals? Finding a way to just reduce Mr. Daymo's power was definitely worthwhile. Jeremy figured he could do alright if he was subjected to wild and nonsensical dreams, as long as he could avoid the horrific ones.

The next night he once again slipped downstairs and slept on the sofa. His dream that night was ghastly. Some unseen assassin was shooting at Jeremy, and the bullets made *whizzing* sounds as they flew past him. The stray bullets hit the ground all around him, creating little puffs of dust as Jeremy ran away. As his legs got heavier and heavier, Jeremy slowed down. He could hear the reports from the gun getting louder. He came to a cliff edge, and even though he tried to stop, Jeremy's body kept moving forward until he slid over the edge. As he fell, Jeremy screamed for help. Before he hit the bottom of the cavern, he woke up. After that nightmare, Jeremy slept in his bed and didn't again try to escape Mr. Daymo by going downstairs.

A few weeks later, Jeremy was sitting in a quiet corner of the playground during lunch recess. It was a warm spring day and Jeremy turned his face towards the noon sun. Instead of playing kickball with the other boys, Jeremy spent more and more recesses sitting in a quiet and remote area, reading, or drawing in a spiral notebook. Rob walked over to Jeremy and said, "Hey."

"Hey," Jeremy responded with not much emotion.

"Aren't we friends no more?" Rob asked, putting his hands on his hips and taking an aggressive stance.

"Huh?"

"You never talk to me. What's the deal? Did someone say something about me?"

"No. No." Jeremy responded absently.

Rob was frustrated. "So you're just too good for me now?" Rob raised his voice and kicked some dirt onto Jeremy. "Is that it?"

"Hey! Cut it out!"

"Sounds like you just don't wanna be friends!" Rob said, kicking some more dirt onto Jeremy.

"Stop it, Rob!" Jeremy leapt to his feet and pushed Rob with both of his hands, causing his friend to fall backwards. Rob looked up with a startled look on his face. Jeremy immediately felt badly about his attack. "Hey, I'm sorry," he said, kneeling down next to Rob. "I don't wanna fight. I...I just want to be friends. Really."

"What's the matter with you?" squawked Rob, slapping away Jeremy's hand.

After pausing briefly to collect his thoughts, Jeremy confessed under his breath, "I have a problem, Rob. A big problem."

Rob's mother had used similar words with him last year when she told him about his granddad's cancer. "Robbie, darling," she said. "Your granddad has a problem. A really big problem." Rob immediately thought that Jeremy was going to tell him that he had cancer, too. "Jeremy, are you saying that you have mela...mellow-nomo?" he asked.

"What's that?"

"It's another word for cancer," explained Rob. "My granddad had it before he died."

"Naw, I don't have cancer. I just have a problem sleeping," Jeremy said. As if on cue, he felt a little twinge in his belly. It wasn't painful, it was just a little reminder from a certain someone that Jeremy was getting close to the electric fence.

"Like, you can't sleep at night?"

"No, I have problems when I sleep." Jeremy chose his words

very carefully because he didn't want to put his best friend in harm's way. "Remember the hospital nurse," he thought. Jeremy also wanted to choose his words carefully because he knew that he would sound like a sissy if he said that his big problem was that he was afraid of nightmares.

"When I sleep, it's like…things happen. I can't explain it very well." Crying in front of another boy was a heinous breach of the Boy Protocol, but Jeremy couldn't prevent a tear from escaping the corner of his eye and rolling down his cheek. Jeremy quickly wiped it away with the back of his hand in what he hoped appeared to be a nonchalant gesture. Rob was frozen in terror at the sight of his best friend's tear. The two boys remained silent for a little bit, neither one knowing what to do or say. Rob was trying to figure out how to react to hearing this intimate confession by his friend. Jeremy was contemplating what more he could say without endangering Rob's life.

Luckily for Jeremy, Rob broke the silence and provided a non-sissy reason for Jeremy's socially unacceptable public display of emotion. "Is this all because of you being in the hospital last year? You know, the surgery and stuff?"

Jeremy saw the opportunity and seized it. "Yeah, yeah I think it's all 'cuz I was in the hospital. It's probably the medicine or the surgery or something like that. They put me under *Anastasia* for my surgery." Both of the boys nodded and seemed satisfied that they had stumbled upon the reason for Jeremy's sullen mood.

"I know surgery's hard," Rob said. "My uncle had surgery and he still ain't right."

Without giving it much thought, Jeremy lamented, "The best sleep I've had all year was at my grandma's house."

"Hey! I got an idea! Do you want to stay overnight at my house tonight?" Rob asked excitedly. "We can get up and watch Saturday morning cartoons together."

With that invitation, Jeremy thought Rob wasn't just his best friend: he was possibly a genius. Jeremy's brain *whirred* as it analyzed Rob's suggestion. Maybe Mr. Daymo's power existed in the entire house (including the sofa downstairs) but did *not* extend beyond Jeremy's house! Rob's house was three blocks away, which Jeremy thought might be outside of Mr. Daymo's zone of power. Jeremy's mood immediately brightened and he asked, "Really? Could we do that? We could have so much fun!"

Jeremy's upbeat energy was infectious and Rob became even more delighted. "I have to ask my parents but you stayed overnight last summer, so I'm sure it would be okay. What about yours?"

"They'll be okay!" Jeremy quickly responded.

The two friends spent the rest of recess talking lively about their plans for the sleepover. By the time the bell rang and everyone went back into the school, the Peace Summit between Rob and Jeremy was concluded, and it was a resounding success.

CHAPTER NINE

The Sleepover

Their parents approved the sleepover, and Jeremy was in high spirits as he walked to Rob's house with his sleeping bag. Each of the boys had a GI Joe, and they played a lengthy improvised scenario wherein the two Joes were looking for buried treasure. They discovered that the treasure was guarded by skeletons, which were played in this scene by green plastic army men. Rob's mom made popcorn and gave each of the boys their own bottle of Vess pop. The boys had a burping contest which led to such loud and crude eruptions that at one point Rob's dad yelled down the stairs for the boys to keep it down. The boys giggled at the thought that they had burped so loudly the adults upstairs had been disturbed. They stayed up very late. It was after midnight when they finally turned out the lights. As they lay in their sleeping bags on the basement floor, they continued to chatter and laugh until they finally dozed off.

Later that night, Jeremy was at school. His regular teacher, Mrs. Markowitz, had been replaced by Captain Kirk from Star Trek, who was wearing his Starfleet uniform. Looking around the classroom, Jeremy thought everything else looked to be in order. At first glance, it appeared his classmates were seated at their assigned desks, just as they had been several hours earlier.

"Today," Captain Kirk announced, "we will be having a test covering what we have learned so far this year." Jeremy panicked because he suddenly realized that he had no earthly idea what subjects they had been studying. As he thought about it further, he came to the disturbing conclusion that for some reason he hadn't attended school for several months. His mind was racing, trying to figure out how he could possibly have missed months of school without anybody noticing. Attendance was taken each morning before lessons began. Shouldn't the school have contacted his parents after he had missed two or three days in a row? How is it that his parents hadn't been alerted that he had failed to go to school? Why had Jeremy decided to simply stop going to school altogether in the first place? What on earth had he been doing every day if he wasn't in school? Jeremy had no idea how he'd been spending his time while skipping school. "This test will determine whether you will continue into the fifth grade. If you fail this test, we will flunk you and you will have to repeat the fourth grade." All of the kids, except Jeremy, said, "Oooooooooh" in a spooky way and then tittered.

Jeremy leaned forward across his desk and shook the shoulders of the kid in front of him. The kid turned around but Jeremy didn't recognize him. Jeremy said frantically, "Tell me what we've been studying! Is it American history? Fractions? The pioneers?" Jeremy thought if he at least had an inkling on the test's basic subject matter he might be able to somehow bluff his way through the test.

"You should have been here at school and then you'd know!" the kid chided and then turned his back on Jeremy in a huff.

Jeremy felt a cold streak of sweat running from the back of his neck all the way down his back into his underwear. He developed a sick, nauseous feeling in his stomach. It wasn't the sharp, gripping pain that heralded the presence of Mr. Daymo. Instead, it was a dull, nauseous ache in his stomach brought about by his dread of the test. He searched his mind, trying to remember if Mrs. Markowitz had ever announced what general subjects they were going to cover that semester but he came up blank. Captain Kirk walked between the desks, distributing test booklets. When the test was dropped onto Jeremy's desk, he thought it sounded like a huge steel door had been slammed shut. Nothing was printed on the first page except the word TEST. After he distributed all of the tests, Captain Kirk said, "Open your test packets and begin." When Jeremy opened the test booklet, he found that the questions were written in a language other than English. It didn't even look like a true language, as it included shapes, numbers, symbols and unrecognizable letters of some kind. Jeremy flipped through the pages and discovered that the entire test was in a bizarre language he could not understand. All of the other students were furiously writing on their mimeographed answer sheets. Jeremy raised his hand and although Captain Kirk was looking right at him, he did not say anything to Jeremy. Waving his hand from side to side frantically did not get the attention of the teacher: his gaze was frozen.

"I think there's a problem with my test. I can't understand it," Jeremy called out to Captain Kirk. The teacher continued to gaze forward and gave no indication he saw or heard Jeremy.

His nausea turned into a particularly sharp and painful stabbing in his lower abdomen, and Jeremy winced when it hit. When he opened his eyes, all of the other students had vanished and Mr. Daymo was leaning against the teacher's desk. Mr. Daymo's dark suit had been replaced with Captain Kirk's uniform of a gold pullover, black slacks and black boots.

"You're not a stupid kid," Captain Daymo said, wagging an index finger at Jeremy. "I wouldn't have chosen you if you were stupid. I don't understand why you aren't doing better at school and at your lessons." Captain Daymo walked to Jeremy's desk and stood over him. "Are you trying to bring attention to yourself?" Jeremy looked up at the man hovering over him and shook his head. "When a kid goes from the upper tier of the class to the bottom of the class, adults get concerned." Captain Daymo put his hands on Jeremy's desk and lowered his head so that it was uncomfortably close to Jeremy's. "That leads to investigation and that leads to little boys making big mistakes. Even small mistakes can be fatal." Jeremy wanted to say he was honestly doing his best but all that came out of his mouth was a little whimper.

"What's that you say?" Captain Daymo asked, leaning his head towards Jeremy.

It was difficult to speak, but Jeremy managed to reply, "Go away. I hate you. Go away."

Captain Daymo shook his head with a disapproving expression on his face. "And after everything I've done for you," he remarked in disgust. He pulled open the top of Jeremy's desk and brought out a pair of headphones. They were black and had two big donut shaped cups that fit over the ears. "Here, put these on," Captain Daymo instructed, tossing the headphones into Jeremy's hands. "If I'm such a bad guy, why would I provide you with knowledge of the things that you need to know?"

After checking to make sure there were no bugs or snakes in the headphone cups, Jeremy did as he was instructed. As soon as he put the headphones on, Jeremy's ears were filled with a loud screeching noise that sounded like a 33 1/3 RPM record album being played at 78 RPM speed. Jeremy tried to pull the headphones off but they had become super-glued to his head and wouldn't budge. As both the speed and the volume of the sounds increased, he violently shook his head from side to side. When Jeremy closed his eyes, he saw thousands of images flash rapidly in his brain. The frantic succession of loud sounds and vivid images pierced Jeremy's brain, and he groaned as the pain increased. Jeremy yelled but he couldn't hear himself over the cacophony of noises assaulting his ears.

"Wake up, Jeremy!" Rob was yelling and shaking Jeremy. "Come on, wake up!"

"Rob?" Jeremy said groggily.

"You're talking in your sleep, man. Really loud!"

Rob's mother called down the stairs, "Are you boys alright?"

"Yeah, mom, we're fine," Rob shouted to his mother.

"Alright, but it's time for sleep. Enough playing. Okay?"

"Sure thing, mom."

They heard her walk away from the top of the stairs.

"So, is that what happens when you sleep?" Rob anxiously asked. As he started to reply, Jeremy felt more than just a twinge in his belly: the pain was so sharp that he bent forward. "Are you okay?" Rob asked with growing concern in his voice.

There was another sharp punctuation of pain and then it was gone. Jeremy tried to assure his best friend by replying in what he hoped sounded like a nonchalant tone. "Yeah, I'm okay. Probably just drank too much pop. Heh!"

Rob relaxed a little. "Man, you were really talking a really lot!"

Jeremy realized at that moment that Rob might be able to provide some helpful information to him. "What did I say? Could ya tell?"

"I don't know. I only woke up because you were talking real loud and then you were slapping your ears really hard. I couldn't understand what you were talking about. You were talking real fast. Too fast for me to get what you were saying."

"You don't remember *anything* I said?" Jeremy asked desperately.

"Naw, it was just all garbled and stuff."

Despite Jeremy asking some additional follow up questions, Rob was unable to tell him anything about what he said in his sleep.

After he returned home, Jeremy thought again about just how far Mr. Daymo's power extended. It apparently included his entire house as well as houses a few blocks away, such as Rob's. Jeremy was left with the inescapable conclusion that the only place that

Jeremy knew for sure that Mr. Daymo's power didn't extend to was his grandparents' house.

"Mom, when will we be going back to Grandma and Grandpa's house?" Jeremy asked that evening.

"Honey, we were just there a few weeks ago," she replied as she cooked their supper. "You know it takes awhile to get there. Remember, before long, it'll be summer vacation and you can go out there for a whole week. Did you and Rob have fun at your sleepover?"

"Yeah," Jeremy said absently, thinking that summer vacation seemed like a very long time away.

Jeremy wasn't the least bit concerned when Rob wasn't at school the following Monday. When he wasn't at school on Tuesday, Jeremy began to wonder if his best friend was okay. He called Rob's house on Tuesday afternoon but there was no answer. On Wednesday, Jeremy was happy to see Rob on the playground before school started.

"You okay, man?" Jeremy asked.

"Yeah. I had a seizure on Saturday night," Rob replied as if he was annoyed at what had happened to him. "It was a bad one. Worst one that I've ever had. I had to stay overnight at the hospital before they'd let me go home."

Jeremy knew his friend had been diagnosed with something called epilepsy, but he'd never seen Rob have a seizure. "Are you going to be okay? Can you still do stuff?"

Rob gestured as if he was pushing something away and said in the same annoyed voice, "Yeah, yeah. It's no big deal. They just have me taking a higher dose of my seizure pills. No big deal. I just can't remember very much about the weekend. I know you came over on Friday night but that's about it."

Rob's tone of voice and his assurances that he was fine eased Jeremy's concerns. With a devilish smile, Jeremy said, "Then you don't remember that I kicked your butt?"

"No, but I *do* remember putting you in a headlock until you cried uncle!" Rob replied, playfully punching Jeremy's arm.

"Oh, so you want some more of a whoopin'?"

The two boys grabbed each other as if they were about to wrestle each other to the ground and then laughed.

* * *

Every Friday morning, Mrs. Markowitz gave a spelling test. The weekly procedure for spelling tests was routine. On Monday morning, she passed out a list of twenty-five words. As the students followed along, she read each word aloud, recited its definition and then used it in a sentence. It was then up to the students to learn to accurately spell each of the words before the test at the end of the week. At Friday morning's test, Mrs. Markowitz read the words aloud, and the students wrote the words on their answer sheets. Jeremy was pretty good at spelling although he found the process of studying for the spelling tests to be tedious. His mother won a spelling bee when she was in elementary school, and it seemed to Jeremy that she took it upon herself to turn Jeremy into the most accurate speller in the world. She had an annoying habit of looking at the list of words when Jeremy got home on Monday and then asking him to spell words at random times during the week.

"Can I have another cookie, Mom?"

"Yes, you can have a cookie," she replied, "if you can spell the word *banana* for me."

"Come on, can't I just have a cookie, mom?"

"Sure, as soon as you correctly spell *banana*!"

Although he'd never admit it to his mother, Jeremy knew this annoying exercise successfully made him more prepared for the weekly spelling tests. On average, he usually got about twenty-three or so of the words correct on the tests. The week after his sleepover at Rob's house had been a difficult week for Jeremy, as his nightly adventures had been particularly intense. After swimming through a pool that had piranhas in it and trying to keep his herd of sheep from being eaten by Wile E. Coyote, the boy was a bit preoccupied. He hadn't sat down and studied any of the words that week. Mom had quizzed him on a couple words during the week but Jeremy had got them wrong. It wasn't until Friday morning before school that Jeremy looked at the list of words that had been given to him on Monday.

The teacher clapped her hands. "Alright everybody. Eyes on your own papers. Let's begin. Number one: *Seaweed*. We saw *seaweed* wash up on the sand at the beach."

Jeremy thought that the first word out of the gate was pretty easy. It was just a long word made up of two little words. *Sea* plus *weed*. He was confident he got that one right and was feeling confident.

"Number two: *Height*. Johnny's *height* was five foot, two inches tall."

Ouch. That one was tough. Was it *hite*? No, it wasn't that easy. Mrs. Markowitz would repeat any of the words that a student requested at the end of the test, so Jeremy decided to think about that one and come back to it later.

"Number three: *Mammal*. A human being is a mammal."

Jeremy wished he had studied the list of words. With the exception of the first word, this list of words was turning out to be brutal. Jeremy decided to go with *mammahl*.

"Number four: *Fleece*. The lamb's *fleece* was white as snow."

Jeremy knew he was in big trouble. Much to his dismay, the words were getting progressively harder. As he pondered whether the answer was *fleese, fleece* or *fleise*, Jeremy thought he could smell cinnamon. He turned around, wondering if someone had just taken out a cinnamon roll to snack on during the test.

"Eyes ahead on your own papers," the teacher said and then

repeated the fourth word at the request of another student.

The strong and unmistakable smell of cinnamon remained in the air but Jeremy couldn't find its source. His stomach felt as though he'd just gone down a big hill on a rollercoaster: it was tingly and floating up towards his chest. He felt a warm, wet gust of air blow into his right ear and he heard, "F-l-e-e-c-e." Jeremy slapped the back of his ear with his right hand and turned around abruptly to see who was whispering into his ear. The kid behind him had his head down and was busily writing on his test sheet.

"Jeremy Bracken, I won't tell you again. Eyes front," Mrs. Markowitz barked, this time louder and with more emphasis.

He turned around and started to speak, "I...I thought..." The voice whispered in his ear again. "F-l-e-e-c-e. It means to trick someone out of money." Jeremy considered what the voice told him. He decided this was indeed the correct spelling and quickly wrote it down just as the teacher was reading the next word.

"Number five: *Pyramid*. The Egyptian king was buried in a *pyramid*."

On his answer sheet, Jeremy wrote *piramid*, crossed it out and then wrote *piramyd*. He knew there was a *y* in the word somewhere but he couldn't remember where it went. Tickling his ear, the voice said, "P-y-r-a-m-i-d. It means to make money from the work of others."

Luckily, the test got a little easier after that, and he didn't need any further assistance whispered to him until the test was almost over. Towards the end, he ran into a couple tough words and he once again received a little assistance. When the test was over, the papers were handed to the student across the aisle and were graded. Mrs. Markowitz read off the correct spellings and the students marked with a check those that were misspelled. Jeremy got twenty-two out of twenty-five correct, which he thought was pretty good considering he hadn't studied.

That night, Jeremy was on a ship that was sinking. People were screaming and crying as the boat's bow pointed downward and the boat started to slide under the water. Jeremy slid down the boat deck and splashed into the ocean. He was a pretty good swimmer but in this dream he had difficulty keeping his head above water. He knew how to tread water and had done it many times but for some unknown reason, his kicking and paddling was not keeping him afloat very well. When his abdomen tightened and spasmed, Jeremy kicked even harder, trying to fight through the pain. Only the back of the ship remained above water. Standing on it was Mr. Daymo, once again wearing his dark suit.

"Jeremy! Hey! Catch this!" he shouted, tossing a white life preserver into the water. Jeremy grabbed onto it and noticed that it was actually an oversized piece of Lifesaver candy. He smelled the crisp peppermint scent coming from the hard candy life preserver. The ship continued to sink, and Mr. Daymo balanced himself so that he remained standing until both the boat and Daymo slid into the water. Just as Mr. Daymo's head was about to go under water he yelled, "There are only so many life preservers on the boat. Don't use them all up." Held up by his candy lifesaver, Jeremy watched for Mr. Daymo to resurface but he never did so.

When Jeremy woke up, he smelled peppermint. He sniffed his hands and they both smelled like peppermint candy. He licked his palms and tasted sharp peppermint flavor on them, as if he had been holding candy canes while he slept.

CHAPTER TEN

An Impossible Mission

Spring is traditionally considered a time for rebirth and growing. For Jeremy, spring was just a continuation of his nightly ordeals. A healthy eight-year-old boy should be putting on weight, but Jeremy weighed the same as he had the previous autumn. His face looked like he was in a perpetual state of having the flu, with very little color in his cheeks. His mother took him back to Dr. Glover shortly after Valentine's Day but a series of blood tests and x-rays were all normal. Spring break was approaching, and Jeremy pestered his mom and dad about taking a trip to see his grandparents. When they did not immediately acquiesce, he became increasingly insistent that he wanted to see his grandparents. However, when his father suggested that his grandparents might be able to stay overnight at *their* house, Jeremy was not enthusiastic about that arrangement.

"What's the difference if they come here or we go there? You'll still get to see them," his father asked.

"I want to go to *their* house," Jeremy said. Then he thought of something else to support his request. "I want to see Smokey, too. Smokey can't ride in grandpa's car. Grandpa wouldn't let him."

"I don't know, son. For us to go back out there, it's a lot of miles on the old car. We'll just have to see."

Mrs. Bracken saw how much the trip meant to Jeremy, and she began to lobby her husband on Jeremy's behalf. Eventually, Jeremy's father approved the family trip. His dad managed to rearrange some projects and get off work early on the Friday of Jeremy's spring vacation. Their car was full of laughing and joking as the three of them travelled across the state. Jeremy fantasized about the bed at his grandparents' house and how it would once again be his safe haven from the nightmares that plagued him.

Grandma prepared a large supper for them, and Jeremy ate heartily. His mother was very pleased to watch her thin and ashen son wolf down multiple helpings of mashed potatoes and fried chicken. The three men watched a television show called *Mission Impossible* while the two women washed the dishes. Jeremy only made it about half way through the one hour TV show before his eyelids started to get heavy. His dad suggested he turn in early, and Jeremy had never been so excited to go to bed as he was that night. He pulled the quilts up to his neck and closed his eyes, knowing that he was going to wake up refreshed.

Jeremy was in a library, but it wasn't his school's library. There were lots of other people in the library, and they all seemed to be very engrossed in what they were reading. He was seated in a study carrel in the corner with a large bluish hardbound book lying in front of him. The title of the book was stamped in gold lettering on the front cover: "*Open Me.*" Jeremy did as the book suggested. Someone had vandalized the book by cutting out the middle of the pages and putting a small tape recorder in the hollowed out area. Jeremy initially was concerned he might get caught with the book and that the head librarian would jump to the conclusion that Jeremy had done this. In the back of his brain, however, he was somehow sure that the head librarian wasn't around and that he could listen to the tape recorder without disturbing the other patrons. He pushed the *play* button.

"Good evening, Mr. Bracken. Your mission, should you choose to accept it, is to save all of these people. If you should fail your mission, the government will deny your existence." Smoke started coming out of the tape recorder, and Jeremy pushed away the book that cradled the smoldering tape recorder. He quickly backed away from the study carrel just as the book and tape recorder blew up. Jeremy shielded his face with his hands and closed his eyes, but he didn't feel any debris from the explosion.

When he dropped his hand and opened his eyes, he was standing on the back of a pickup truck in a desert. People were holding out their arms towards the truck. The hot air was full of their wails and cries for help. Instead of emaciated people dressed in rags, the crowd consisted of real people and fictional characters he recognized. As he looked out over the huge crowd that surrounded the truck, he saw a menagerie that included Mr. Spock, Rob, Bugs Bunny, The Joker, kids from his class, and the Grinch. They were all calling out to Jeremy by name, pleading for assistance.

"What...what do you want from me?" Jeremy stammered, holding his empty hands out to them.

Some of the people who were closest to the truck began to push it, causing the truck to rock from side to side. Howard Cosell and Joe Namath lowered their shoulders and pushed against one side of the truck bed. On the other side, Principal Wohlers and the Nestle Quik rabbit grabbed the truck's fender as if they were trying to pick up the vehicle. As he tried to keep his balance and not fall out of the truck, he felt like he was standing on a small rowboat that was being jostled by large ocean waves. As if on cue, he was now in a little rowboat and all of the people around him were trying to swim. The unruly crowd was busily trying to keep their heads above water. Some of them would periodically drop below the water and then reemerge. During these efforts, they were still shouting pleas for assistance to Jeremy. He looked in the small boat, but there were no life preservers.

"I don't have anything to give you!" Jeremy yelled helplessly.

Jeremy and the crowd were then back in the desert. When Jeremy looked down at the bed of the truck, he saw a stack of gleaming tin cans. They looked like the typical silver cans that were found at the grocery store except they didn't have any labels. Jeremy picked up cans and tossed them into the crowd. There was a loud cheer from the crowd as Jeremy threw can after can into the mass of humanity. Jeremy bent down and started tossing cans behind him without taking the time to see where they were going. When he had thrown the last can out of the truck, he stood up and looked at the crowd. There were just as many people begging for help as there was before.

"That's it," Jeremy announced, once again showing his empty hands to the people. "There are no more cans in here."

"We want the tomatoes!" his uncle Ted yelled, and then everyone starting chanting "To-ma-toes! To-ma-toes!"

When Jeremy looked around, he saw a bushel basket of tomatoes sitting on top of the truck's cab. Holding the basket by the handles, Jeremy launched the entire haul of the tomatoes in the direction of his uncle. Uncle Ted and the people standing next to him snagged the tomatoes out of the air and cheered.

"I don't have any more!" Jeremy said to the crowd, holding the basket out so they could see that it was empty.

"Give us the corn!" Reggie Jackson yelled, which caused the rest of the crowd to chant, "Corn! Corn!"

"I don't have any..." Jeremy began to say and then noticed he was ankle deep in ears of corn. Without hesitation, Jeremy tossed aside the empty basket, bent down and started throwing ears of corn into the mass of people. Jeremy threw ears of corn into the crowd like he was a well-oiled machine. Even when it felt like a sharp long knife had been jabbed into his midsection, Jeremy continued to distribute the corn. When there were no ears of corn left, he blindly threw handfuls of loose corn kernels behind him. He thought to himself that he must have been doing a good job because the crowd had become quiet. With just a few handfuls of corn remaining in the truck bed, Jeremy looked up to see if the crowd had been satisfied. The truck was no longer surrounded by people begging for help. Lying on the ground around the truck were corpses. With his mouth gaping, Jeremy saw hundreds of bodies lying motionless on the sand. As he surveyed the area, he saw that Rob's mom and dad were dead. So was Johnny Bench. And Porky the Pig. And Tommy from down the street. His eyes were drawn to the big round head of Charlie Brown's corpse. When he looked at Charlie Brown, Jeremy noticed he was lying right next to Jeremy's mom.

When he saw his mother lying in the sand, Jeremy tried to jump out of the bed of the pickup truck but his feet were stuck. He bent down and grabbed his ankles but his feet wouldn't move. "Mom! Mom!" he cried. In a fit of frustration, he picked up a handful of corn kernels and threw them at the window on the back of the truck's cab. The window shattered with a crash as the glass shards made a tinkling noise when they fell into the truck's metal bed. Jeremy looked up and managed to twist his body a little but he was still tethered to the truck bed. "Mom!" he shouted again, straining to get himself positioned where he could grab something and pull himself out of the truck bed. No matter how much effort he made, he was unable to move his feet. When he tried to untie his shoes, he found the laces were welded together.

One of the dead bodies about 50 yards away stood up. Jeremy wasn't the least bit surprised when a thin man wearing a dark suit rose from the corpses strewn across the sand. Mr. Daymo casually brushed the sand off his dark suit and walked towards the truck. As he trudged through the deep white sand, he withdrew a cigarette from the pack kept in the breast pocket of his jacket and lit it with his silver lighter. When he reached the truck, Jeremy noticed that the man's breathing was labored. Jeremy thought he heard some whistling sounds when Mr. Daymo breathed.

"Walking in sand can make you feel older than you are and about a hundred pounds heavier," Mr. Daymo remarked, pointing with his lit cigarette at the tracks in the sand he'd just made.

"My... mom..." Jeremy whimpered, still trying to free himself from the truck bed.

"Yes, your mother. Are you getting all this?" Mr. Daymo asked, waving his cigarette over his head.

"I...I...tried..." Jeremy said and then trailed off. He made an effort to pull his feet out of his shoes without loosening the shoelaces, but that didn't work either. Jeremy looked up and stared towards his mother.

Mr. Daymo sighed in a disgusted manner and glared at Jeremy. The boy didn't see the man's disappointed glare because Jeremy was focused solely on his mother. After sighing a second time, Mr. Daymo took a long drag from his cigarette and then exhaled towards the boy standing in the truck bed. As soon as the cloud of smoke reached Jeremy, his feet were no longer glued to the truck's bed. The smoke smelled like vinegar, and Jeremy instantly thought of the PAAS Easter egg coloring kit he and his mother used. Jeremy whipped around and looked behind the truck but there were no longer any people lying on the sand. "Mom!" He turned himself around and glanced at the entire area around the truck but there were no bodies anywhere.

"Where did she go? Is she okay?" Jeremy asked Mr. Daymo. The man in the dark suit gave Jeremy a sour look and then turned his back on the boy. As the man took a few steps, Jeremy shouted, "Hey! You!" He kicked the side of the truck bed and it made a *gong* sound that caused Mr. Daymo to turn back to Jeremy.

Mr. Daymo took another long pull from his cigarette and spoke while he exhaled the vinegar smelling smoke towards the boy. "Did you know, Jeremy, that some parasites will feed on their host so much that they eventually kill it? Imagine that. You can bring about your own death simply by overindulging. That's quite a bitter meal, don't you think?"

He flicked the cigarette towards the truck bed, and it bounced off of Jeremy's chest. Bright orange sparks erupted from Jeremy's shirt. He brushed his chest frantically until he was sure he wasn't on fire. Mr. Daymo once more turned his back on Jeremy and began walking slowly in the other direction through the sand.

"Wait! Where's my mom? What'd you do with her?" Mr. Daymo kept walking and did not favor Jeremy with a reply. "Hey! I asked you a question!"

The man kept walking.

Jeremy looked for something to throw at Mr. Daymo, but all that was left in the truck bed were some leftover corn kernels. He picked up a handful of corn and threw it at the man who was walking away from him. "Hey!" When Jeremy tried to jump out of the truck and chase the man, Jeremy suddenly felt very, very tired. His clothes felt as heavy as lead and he gently lowered himself into the truck bed.

"I've been really tired lately. I'll just lay down here in this truck for a minute and then I'll catch up with him," he thought to himself.

"I'm so tired," he said softly as he laid his head on the metal truck bed. He seemed to be moving in slow motion as his fingers played with some of the corn kernels that remained in the bed. "Mom. I'll find you," Jeremy whispered as he fell asleep.

When Jeremy opened his eyes, his mother was sitting on the bed, gently humming a tune. Jeremy didn't immediately recognize where he was. It was a strange bedroom, definitely not his own. He was surprised to see his dead mother, and he recoiled when she laid her hand on his cheek. "What did..." was all he managed to say.

"It's okay, honey," she said, "it was just another bad dream.

Remember?"

Jeremy didn't initially believe he'd been dreaming. He distinctly saw his mother's corpse baking in a desert alongside hundreds of other unfortunates. There was a mob, and it was made up of people he knew. He tried to help them. He tried his best, but they all died. He saw it happen. It was real. There was a part of his brain that questioned whether the entire incident in the truck was nothing but make-believe. Could that be true? Was that entire sequence of disturbing events nothing more than a demented and cruel dream? In this case, it sounded too good to be true. Could he be so lucky to lose his mother and then get a reprieve? Could she really be alive and well? Jeremy looked at the woman who was seated next to him with tears in his eyes. His voice was full of both hope and fear when he said to her in a hesitant voice, "Mom? Is that really you? Really and truly?"

She smiled broadly and pulled him to her. "Of course it is, honey. I'm here for you. And look," she pulled away from Jeremy so that he could see, "here's dad, too! We're both here for you, my brave boy!"

His dad leaned down and asked, "Was it a bad one, sport?"

As bad as the nightmare had been, Jeremy felt like he had won the lottery. He had lost his mother earlier that night and now she was back. Jeremy's tears of relief ran down his cheeks, and both of his parents wrapped their arms around him.

"It's okay, hon, all of us are safe," his mother assured him.

"I don't...I don't want nothing bad to happen to you," Jeremy sobbed. "Never."

His father smiled a little and reassured his son. "Don't worry about us, sport. We're okay. Honest Injun."

Jeremy was so full of relief and happiness that it was hard for him to relax and go back to sleep. His mother offered to stay in the room with him, but Jeremy told her that he would be alright. Jeremy was concerned that if he fell asleep before she did, she might hear him say things that could endanger her. The only way his parents would be safe was in another room, unable to hear their son talk in his sleep. She pulled the quilts all the way up to his neck and kissed him on the tip of his nose.

As he stared at the ceiling, he thought about how vivid and realistic the truck dream had been and how when he awoke, he was absolutely sure that his mother was dead. A defiant voice in his head suggested that she *was* dead and that *this* was the dream. He told that voice it was wrong and it should shut up.

As he started to drift off to sleep, he shifted his body and laid on his right side. When he did so, he felt something move in the little pocket that was on his pajama top. His dad used to joke that the makers of boys' pajamas thought that the wearers would need a place to put the pens and pencils that they would be using while they slept. Jeremy reached into the pocket and felt a couple small hard things that were each about the size of a jellybean. "Did I leave jellybeans in my pocket?" He squeezed them between his fingers and there was no give. There was enough moonlight that Jeremy could hold them up and see what they were without getting up to turn on the light. He had three kernels of corn in his hand. Jeremy was repelled by the kernels and quickly threw them across the room. He pulled the quilts up to his eyes. His eyes continuously darted around the room. He was still awake when the sun rose that morning.

CHAPTER ELEVEN

A Drastic Plan

The trip home was not nearly as fun and cheerful as the one earlier that year. As the car pulled onto the highway, Jeremy was preoccupied with a concern that the terrible truck dream would return and he would see his mother die once again. To make sure this didn't happen, he pledged that he would never sleep again. Despite his best efforts to stay awake, however, Jeremy slept most of the way home.

As they pulled into their driveway, his mother woke him up by squeezing his cheek. When he realized he had slept for hours, he nervously asked his parents if he had said anything while he slept. Thankfully, they reported that although they heard Jeremy mumble some things under his breath, they couldn't make out anything he said.

Jeremy came to the unfortunate but inescapable conclusion that Mr. Daymo's control over his dreams was not limited by geography. The nightly caller had proven that his zone of power reached even into Grandma and Grandpa's house.

Famous psychologists such as Dr. Ford Freud have written about how the brain responds when a person experiences abject failure. If a patient loses all hope, often all that remains are the ghosts of his grand plans and his optimistic goals. He is so empty that he seeks *something… anything* to fill the void where hope once resided. Studies show this is often how we end up with alcoholics, drug addicts, gamblers, joggers and avid collectors of stuffed animals. For a desperate few, the loss of hope drives the patient even

　　　　　　　A CURE FOR NIGHTMARES

harder to find a hidden solution to their problem, even if the prospect of success looks hopeless.

In Jeremy's case, he had a weak but persistent feeling that all hope wasn't yet lost. There was something in the boy's brain that kept suggesting there just *had* to be something that he could do to overcome his nightmares. Almost swallowed up by his despair was a reticent voice in the back of his mind, saying that the situation wasn't completely hopeless. That voice resolutely claimed that there *had* to be something Jeremy had overlooked when devising ways to thwart Mr. Daymo. All Jeremy had to do is recognize it and execute it.

Weeks later, Jeremy suddenly came up with a new battle plan. At supper, Jeremy's mother put a slice of Swiss steak with cooked tomatoes on his plate. Jeremy didn't have much of an appetite but he put a little piece of cooked tomato in his mouth.

"Oh, I almost forgot the veggy!" his mother said and retrieved a small pan from the stove. When she put a large spoonful of corn on Jeremy's plate, a bank of stadium lights were flipped on in his brain. All of a sudden Jeremy was thinking very clearly. Jeremy picked up a couple kernels of corn and contemplated them as he held them in his hand.

"Don't play with your food," his dad said, cutting into the tough piece of discount meat his wife had prepared.

"Corn," Jeremy said absently.

"Yeah, don't play with your corn, either."

"The peppermint smell on my hands," Jeremy said softly, deep in his thoughts.

"Are you okay, honey?" his mother asked. "You look pale all of a sudden."

The void in Jeremy was suddenly filled with hope once again and he felt energized. "No, nothing wrong, Mom," he said cheerfully dropping the corn onto his plate, "I just thought of something really good!"

"Oh, that's nice. Something you can tell us about?" she asked.

"Well...just a project for school. I just came up with a great idea!"

"Good food will always help you come up with good ideas," his dad remarked, giving a wink to his wife. She blushed a little and smiled at him. He moved his eyebrows up and down, and she blushed a little more.

After supper, it seemed his parents were extremely enthusiastic when Jeremy asked if he could go to the park. They thought the idea was a very good one and suggested Jeremy go right away before it got dark. This gave Jeremy quiet time to think about his next action.

As he thought about his dreams, he concluded that the peppermint smell on his hands and the kernels of corn in the pocket of his pajamas were keys that could unlock himself from his nightly prison. The solution had been there all along but he'd been slow to realize it. Jeremy had slept poorly for months and he thought this was the likely reason it took him so long to figure out what he should do next. What he was going to do was certainly drastic and likely dangerous. When you thought all hope was lost, however, you will grab tightly onto whatever helps tamp down your despair.

Jeremy saw his father's pistol once when he was about six. His dad had the weapon disassembled on the kitchen table and was using an old toothbrush to clean the small metal components.

"What's that?" young Jeremy asked, pointing at the metal parts strewn about on the table.

"Nothing. Just something to help me protect my best girl and best boy! Now you run along."

Jeremy did as he was told and ran into the living room. He sat on the end of the couch so he could see the TV as well as the kitchen table. While he pretended to be watching television, he watched intently as his father snapped together several metal pieces in order to make a gun. His mother walked into the kitchen, and young Jeremy could tell she was not fond of the pistol. She looked into the living room and caught Jeremy peering into the kitchen. His mother swooped into the living room making helicopter sounds, picked up her son, and took him outside. The young mother played with her son for awhile, hoping he'd forget about what he had seen. Jeremy never talked to his parents about the gun, but he never forgot about it.

Honestly, Jeremy wasn't sure his father still had the gun. Whether his dad still had it and whether the gun was kept in the house were questions Jeremy didn't know the answer to. For all he knew, it could have been sold or given away years ago. To find out the answers to these questions, Jeremy needed some time alone in the house so he could look for the gun. He needed not just time but *quality* time when he could earnestly search the house. It made sense to do this search when his father was at work, since that took care of half of his problem. The issue was when his mother would be out of the house while his dad was at work.

The following week, Jeremy made a point to come directly home after school. He lurked around the house, keeping tabs on his mother. As his mother used the vacuum cleaner on the main floor of the house, Jeremy searched through some boxes stored in the basement. When his mother's attention was focused on making supper, he checked the living room, bathroom, and tool shed. Although he was pretty sure the gun wouldn't be kept in one of these common areas, it was easy to conclusively check those places off of his list of places to search. He needed time and privacy to check the remaining areas.

By the time Jeremy returned home from school, his mother was usually making the initial preparations for their evening meal. There was no way he could conduct the remainder of his search with his mother still in the house. It was a small two bedroom house with a main floor and a small basement. If his mother decided to check on him, he would have 10 or 15 seconds before she was standing next to him. If he was searching someplace that he should not, he wouldn't have enough time to avoid being seen. Over the following days, Jeremy watched for an opportunity. On Friday afternoon, Jeremy came home to find his mother in the garden.

As she was spreading handfuls of fertilizer over the ground, she warned, "Don't get too close to me: I'm a manure spreader!" It appeared to Jeremy that his mom had just started the task. "If you're going to be in the house, will you answer the phone if anyone calls? I want to try to get this all done and get cleaned up before your father gets home. He's taking us out for hamburgers tonight!"

"How long do you think it will take you?" Jeremy asked, surveying the size of the garden.

"An hour or so. If I'm not back in the house by 4:45 will you come get me, sweetie?"

"Sure, mom. I'm going to watch cartoons and Gilligan's Island," Jeremy replied.

"There's a banana on the counter and you can have *one* oatmeal cookie for a snack."

Jeremy rushed into the house. He turned on the television and watched Looney Tunes for a few minutes, contemplating whether he had the courage to continue his search for the gun. His heart was beating faster than usual. He got up from the couch and looked out the back window, where he saw his mother working diligently in the garden at the far end of their backyard.

Jeremy thought about the two places he had yet to search. There was a place in the kitchen to search and if it wasn't there, he would have to venture into his parents' bedroom. A voice in his brain told him not to go on this expedition. "She'll come in the

114   A CURE FOR NIGHTMARES

house and you'll get caught for sure! You'll be in big trouble! You'll probably not get to have hamburgers tonight! You're not going to find anything in the first place, so don't do it!" Jeremy resolved that he had to ignore that voice and try to find the gun.

The first place he looked was in the big cabinet over the refrigerator. This was the same cabinet where his mother sequestered his Halloween candy. It was so high up even his mother had to use a step stool to reach it. A year ago, his father set aside a couple packages of firecrackers from July 4th to shoot on New Year's Eve. They were kept in this cabinet and Jeremy was told not to get into that cabinet under any circumstances. Since firecrackers were dangerous and they made an explosion, he thought maybe that was where his father kept the gun. He dragged a chair over to the refrigerator and got on his tip toes to open the cabinet. The inside smelled stale and musty, probably because it was hard to reach and was rarely opened. The only thing that was in the cabinet was a punchbowl and a lot of punch glasses shaped like teacups. Jeremy pushed the punchbowl aside a little so he could look behind it but he saw nothing but dust.

The last place to look was his parent's bedroom. Jeremy knew very little about the room where his parents slept. He vaguely remembered sleeping with his parents once or twice when he was very little, but that was about it. There simply hadn't been any reason for Jeremy to spend a lot of time in the bedroom. Now that he was standing in the doorway, he took a moment to carefully survey the area. Mom had made the bed and there were no dirty clothes on the floor. In the Penney's catalog, there were photographs of meticulously clean rooms with furniture and bedspreads for sale. His parents' bedroom looked tidy enough to be in the catalog.

The most logical place to hide something in a bedroom, Jeremy thought, was under the bed. Taking his Cub Scout flashlight from his pocket, Jeremy knelt down beside the bed and pulled up the corner of the quilted comforter. There were a few shoe boxes under the bed which Jeremy fished out for inspection. On the boxes, his mother had written "old boots" and "old shoes" and that is exactly what was in them. After carefully returning the boxes to their original position, Jeremy got off floor and turned his attention to the nightstands. He figured the nightstand on his father's side of the bed was where his father could get to the gun quickly if there was an intruder during the night. After peeking out the window to make sure his mother was still in the garden, Jeremy opened the drawer to his father's nightstand.

On top, there were some brochures for fishing lodge rentals which Jeremy moved aside. A thrill of discovery surged through his body when he saw the pistol lying in the drawer. The barrel and trigger were black like coal, and it had a dark brown wooden handle. As the initial excitement of discovery subsided, Jeremy felt fear.

He hesitatingly reached towards the gun as if it was a cobra ready to strike. The first time his fingertips touched the handle, he pulled hand back quickly. He was anxious to get the gun, but he was also afraid of it. Once again he slowly reached towards the gun. As he touched the handle, Jeremy became aware that loud drums reverberating in his head were beating in time with his furiously thumping heart. When he tried to pick it up, he was amazed at how heavy it was. On television, cowboys toted around their guns as if they were as light as paper. He was scared that he'd drop the heavy pistol, so he used two hands to hold the gun: one on the handle and one on the barrel.

Just like the ones the TV cowboys used, the pistol had a barrel shaped area that held bullets. He fumbled with the gun, trying to figure out how to snap the cylinder out so that he could check to see if there were bullets in the chambers. Despite rolling the gun over in his hands and inspecting it carefully, he couldn't seem to figure it out. He noticed, however, that if he pointed the gun at himself, he could see some bullet heads peeking from the chambers.

Jeremy thought he heard something in the house. When he closed the nightstand drawer, he did so too firmly and it made a loud hollow noise. "Shhhh!" he hissed at the drawer. He ran to his room and slid the pistol between his twin mattress and the box spring. He then sat on the bed and tried to look casual. If his grandmother had seen him, she would have said he looked like the cat that ate the canary. After sitting like a statue for a few minutes, Jeremy walked down the hall, through the kitchen and to the back screen door. His mother was cleaning her garden tools with the back yard hose.

"Can you give me a little help?" she asked when she saw him in the doorway.

Jeremy helped her finish and then hung the utensils up in their rusty little tool shed.

"You're my little helper today!" she commented. Jeremy smiled but didn't say anything. His mind was focused on the gun that was hidden in his bedroom and the deed he intended to commit later that night.

As he watched television with his parents, he kept playing out in his head what he planned to do. Even though it was Friday night, Jeremy volunteered to go to bed at his regular bedtime. Once he was in bed and the bedroom door was shut, he reached under the mattress and withdrew the gun. It still felt very heavy and he once again held it tightly with his two little hands. Dr. Glover had told him to think happy thoughts before falling asleep. Tonight, he thought hard about the fact that he had a gun.

Over and over, he told himself, "I've got a gun in my hands. I've got a gun in my hands." The moment he fell asleep, he wanted his final thought to be, "I've got a gun in my hands." Just like the peppermint smell and kernels of corn that he brought with him from his dreams, he was going to bring something with him to his dream tonight.

All of the anticipation and nervousness kept Jeremy from becoming drowsy. He was still wide awake when he heard his parents go to bed. He closed his eyes and tried to will himself to go to sleep but he remained awake. Could someone go through an entire night and not sleep at all? He didn't think so and this helped to assure him that he'd definitely fall asleep at some point. He didn't know how long he laid in his bed. Jeremy was coming to the conclusion he was never going to be able to fall asleep that night. He still had the pistol in his hands when he finally nodded off.

When Jeremy walked through the swinging double doors of the saloon, he saw that it was a busy night. There were several cowboys sitting at the tables and Jeremy nodded politely at those he recognized. James West and Artemis Gordon from *The Wild Wild West* were talking to Marshal Matt Dillon from *Gunsmoke*. All three of them held up their beer mugs to salute Jeremy. The Lone Ranger and Tonto were in an obviously heated discussion with Yosemite Sam but Jeremy couldn't hear what they were arguing about. Jeremy climbed up on a barstool next to a cowboy who was wearing an impressive six gallon hat. And a red clown nose.

"Howdy, pardner," the cowpoke said to Jeremy, tipping his hat.

"Hi," Jeremy said, nodding at the cowboy. The cowboy with the clown nose excused himself and walked to the piano, where he and the pianist starting singing a song that Jeremy didn't recognize.

"What'll it be?" asked ex-President Richard Nixon, who had apparently become this dusty saloon's barkeep after leaving office.

Before Jeremy could reply, his stomach was gripped with pain. He grabbed onto the bar to steady himself and dug his fingernails into the wood until the cramping subsided.

"You alright?" the barkeep asked. "What's your poison?"

"I…I don't know," Jeremy said. "Um…whiskey?"

"Coming up!" The barkeep turned his back and started a blender. He poured what looked like a chocolate shake into a tall fluted glass and sprayed whipped cream onto the top. "One whiskey, just as you ordered," ex-president Nixon said as he set the glass on the bar in front of Jeremy. As Jeremy reached for the glass, most of the lights in the bar went out and the music stopped playing. Everyone stopped talking, and the room quickly went from being as noisy as a honky-tonk to as quiet as a tomb. A tall cowboy wearing a dark business suit and a black cowboy hat walked through the double doors. Lighting a cigarette with a metal lighter, he made a beeline towards Jeremy. No one made a noise as the man strode directly up to Jeremy's barstool and glared down on him. A glimmering silver star was pinned to the lapel of his dark jacket.

"Howdy, cowboy," Sheriff Daymo said. "I'm the sheriff 'round these parts. What're you doin' in my town?"

Jeremy wanted to provide a witty retort, but he suddenly couldn't remember how to speak. His brain was telling his mouth to say something clever to the town's lawman, but his mouth didn't move. All of the hairs on his arms felt like they were standing on end, and his heart was racing. Jeremy stole a glance down to his leather gun belt and saw that he had a pistol cradled in the holster. He recognized from the color of the wooden grip sticking out of his holster that he was carrying his dad's revolver. Jeremy quickly looked back up at the sheriff, hoping the lawman hadn't seen him check his weapon.

"How can you tell the number of friends and the number of enemies you have in a crowded room? Got any guesses?" Sheriff Daymo asked. When Jeremy didn't reply, the sheriff said, "False smiles are like swamps: they may look sturdy, but you'll sink if you don't make the right step. Ever thought about that, my young friend?"

Jeremy tried to focus on what he needed to do. His right hand moved slowly down to his holster while Jeremy's eyes remained locked on Mr. Daymo's. A frantic voice in Jeremy's head interrupted his train of thought by yelling, "What a minute! You can't shoot a sheriff! He's the law!"

Jeremy's hand stopped moving as he thought about this for a moment. A second voice in his head replied to the first one, "Yeah, but he isn't *really* a sheriff. Shoot him!"

The first voice responded cheerfully, "Oh, okay. Forget I said anything."

Jeremy's right hand resumed its slow trek down to his holster. When Jeremy's fingers reached the top of the holster, they didn't touch anything that felt like the grip of a gun. Jeremy definitely did *not* want to look down at his holster, so he groped around the top of his holster with his hand as he continued to match the sheriff's icy stare. Instead of a hard pistol grip, Jeremy felt something soft and round between his fingers, about the size a tennis ball. It was squishy when he squeezed it. This wasn't how it was supposed to happen. Jeremy had planned to reach into the holster, pull his gun out and shoot the man wearing the dark business suit.

All of the lights in the saloon came back on, and a jukebox started playing the Eric Clapton song, "*I Shot the Sheriff.*" The words in the song were garbled and didn't even sound like English. It sounded as if Mr. Clapton forgot the lyrics and he was just making up words as he went along. The only words Jeremy could understand were in the song's refrain, which clearly described how Mr. Clapton had shot the sheriff.

Jeremy thought to himself, "Who played that song on the jukebox?! It's going to warn Sheriff Daymo what I'm planning to do!" Now that someone had tipped off Sheriff Daymo by playing that stupid song, time was even more of the essence. Jeremy was left with no choice but to take a look down at his holster and find the gun's handle. When he looked down, he saw that his fingers weren't touching the grip of his father's pistol. Between his fingers was a large tomato. There was no gun in his holster any longer, just a ripe tomato. Jeremy stared at the tomato in utter disbelief. "But…." he said under his breath.

Sheriff Daymo asked, "You looking for *this*, cowboy?" Jeremy's eyes shot up and the sheriff was holding his father's gun, the barrel pointed menacingly at Jeremy. He had watched enough cowboy shows to know that the sheriff "had the drop on him". Sheriff Daymo started to laugh as he effortlessly spun the revolver in a circle around his index finger.

Jeremy concentrated hard and he silently repeated the mantra in his head: "I have a gun in my hands." After repeating it several times, Jeremy looked at his hands. They were empty.

"I thought we were past this stage in our development," Sheriff Daymo lamented, who stopped playfully twirling the gun on his finger and once again pointed the barrel at Jeremy's chest. To emphasize his point, Sheriff Daymo shook the gun in front of Jeremy's face and chided, "*This* was your master plan? Your dad's gun?"

Jeremy was too scared to reply. He was shivering all over as if he was outside in the cold without a coat. Jeremy's eyes were focused intently on the barrel of the gun, expecting fire to erupt from the end just as soon as the sheriff pulled the trigger. "Did you honestly believe that this gun was going to bring an end to your lessons? Did you *really* and truly believe you were going to be able to shoot me? Come on! You're smarter than that, Jeremy."

There was no reply from Jeremy. The shivering boy was at a complete loss as what to do or say at that moment. Jeremy was sure he was about to find out what really happens when you die in your dreams. After a few silent moments, the sheriff continued to berate Jeremy.

"These aren't toys, Jeremy! Bad things happen to little boys who play with these, don't you know that?" Jeremy managed to nod just a little.

Waving the barrel of the gun in front of Jeremy's face, Sheriff Daymo said, "You've got the gun in your hand, you're looking down the barrel and then…" A red flag popped out of the end of the barrel with the word "BANG" printed on it. "And then *oops*, you've got yourself a dead kid. That's not good for anybody." He shook the gun again. "Why would you want to put your life at risk?"

A *ding* sound went off in Jeremy's head. There was something that Sheriff Daymo just said that was important. Jeremy's young brain churned as it tried to separate the valuable wheat from the useless chaff. His brain was still dealing with the failure of his plan, and this was getting in the way of identifying the very important thing that Sheriff Daymo just told him. Jeremy tried to clear his mind and focus only on what Sheriff Daymo said. The answer was so simple and when Jeremy figured it out, he couldn't wait to unleash it on Sheriff Daymo.

"Okay, if I can't shoot you, what if I shot myself? Like you said, a dead kid is not good for anybody," Jeremy said confidently as he smiled mischievously at the sheriff.

Jeremy's words broke through Sheriff Daymo's veneer, and he saw that the sheriff was concerned. Jeremy had never seen a scintilla of doubt during all of his dealings with Mr. Daymo until that moment. On every other occasion, Mr. Daymo had always been very self-assured and in complete control. For the very first time, the roles had reversed. It appeared to Jeremy that the student now had the teacher on the ropes, and Jeremy was relishing it. Jeremy savored the doubt and concern that he saw swimming around in Mr. Daymo's eyes. The longer Jeremy looked into Mr. Daymo's concerned eyes, the bigger Jeremy's smile became.

"That's a rather wry smile," the sheriff quipped.

"What's a wry smile?"

"It's a kind of bread." The two cowboys kept their eyes locked

A CURE FOR NIGHTMARES

on each other for a few silent moments. "You know this is *my* realm and *I* am in control," Sheriff Daymo said, trying to sound self-assured.

Jeremy thought about that statement. Like a baseball player who is on a hitting streak, Jeremy was seeing every pitch very clearly and he was hitting them out of the park. "Well then, what if I use it in the real world? You know, where *I'm* in control? What if I shoot myself after I wake up?"

The sheriff tried to maintain his poker face, but Jeremy could tell that the man was flustered. Mr. Daymo's eyes had forsaken him, and Jeremy could see the man was frantically trying to process this information. After a few moments of doubt, however, the man's shattered veneer repaired itself, and Sheriff Daymo's cool self-assured exterior returned.

"Have it your way, cowboy," Sheriff Daymo said, matching Jeremy's wry smile with one of his own. He held the gun handle out to Jeremy. The "BANG" flag was gone. "Here. Take it. If that's what you really want," the sheriff instructed.

Jeremy cautiously reached for the gun but decided that he really didn't want it. Jeremy made a fist and Sheriff Daymo thumped it with the pistol handle, trying to force his hand to take the gun. Against his will, Jeremy's hand opened and grasped the gun. As soon as he grabbed the gun's handle, the red "BANG" flag came out of the barrel and Jeremy heard a thundering *BOOM*.

Jeremy was in his bed and his ears were ringing. He couldn't hear anything except a loud whistling noise in his ears.

It smelled like something was burning.

It smelled like the Fourth of July block party.

It smelled like a long strip of firecrackers had gone off in his bedroom.

His mother and father were trying to reach their son with such desperation that they ran into each other and spilled into the bedroom. As soon as his mother saw the gun, she started screaming and crying at the same time. Jeremy couldn't hear his mother's cries because his ears were ringing, so he watched her perform a pantomime of a woman in distress. His father had his arms in the air and his mouth was open. His dad was yelling, but Jeremy couldn't hear him. Rushing over to the bed, his father pulled off the bedspread and Jeremy saw that portions of it were smoking. His mom was still at the door, her head buried in her hands as if she was too terrified to look at the scene. Jeremy felt something burning his inner thigh and when he looked down, he saw the barrel of the pistol resting against his leg. His father grabbed the gun and looked at it quizzically as if he had no idea what it was. He held the gun like a chimp would hold a telephone, moving it around in his hands as if trying to determine what it was.

Jeremy saw that the bullet fired from his father's gun ripped through the bedding but it luckily hadn't hit Jeremy. Other than the loss of hearing, Jeremy was physically unharmed. Once his father realized his son was unharmed, he was able to tend to his wife who was still inconsolable. Eventually he ushered her to their bedroom and convinced her to take two sleeping pills.

It was a few hours later before Jeremy could hear anything. During that time, Jeremy had a lot of thinking to do. What was Jeremy going to do now? Since he was convinced he was going to successfully assassinate Mr. Daymo, Jeremy hadn't seriously considered what his next step would be if he failed to shoot and kill Mr. Daymo. Jeremy wasn't thinking very clearly at that point because he was so despondent about his plan's failure. Was the path of Jeremy's life that had been dictated by the man in the dark suit inviolate and unchangeable? When he was really old, like in his thirties, would he still be enduring the nightly visits? Jeremy's pride was damaged and he felt like a failure. He should have been able to figure his way out of this mess.

A CURE FOR NIGHTMARES

Instead of focusing on another way to bring an end to the nightly visitations by Mr. Daymo, Jeremy needed to figure out how he was going to come out of this disaster with the least amount of punishment. "Can I be put in jail for this?" he thought to himself. "Are my parents going to call the police and have me hauled down to the city jail? If I was in jail, would I still go to school? Is there such a thing as *Jail School*?"

Number one on the list of questions he'd be asked would be, "Why did you take the gun?" There was no way he could claim the gun ended up in his bed by happenstance. Neither chance nor serendipity would be a plausible explanation. There was no way to claim the pistol had been planted on him by a third party. He knew he couldn't tell his parents the truth, otherwise they would all be in danger. Remember the nurse with the brown eyes. In the end, it seemed to Jeremy that the best answer to the question was the truth, minus some of the details. When his father sat down with him on the couch, Jeremy confessed tearfully that he knew he'd done something wrong, but he had a reason for doing so.

"I wanted to protect myself when I was in my dreams," he told his father. Jeremy was careful not to identify a particular person or thing from which he needed protection. He was also very careful to always refer to the gun as a means of *protection*. He was cautious not to tell his father that he'd actually planned to hunt and hopefully kill something that haunted him in his dreams. His dad showed little emotion as Jeremy explained his rationale and Jeremy wasn't sure if the story was going to have any effect on the punishment that would eventually be meted out.

In the early morning hours, Jeremy fell asleep on the couch while being cradled by his dad. As they slept, his father's arms would periodically tense and pull his son tightly against his chest.

For the entire weekend, it became clear to Jeremy that his parents had made a pact to keep him under constant observation.

Even when he used the bathroom, the door was kept open, which Jeremy found to be weird and gross. He heard snippets of several telephone conversations his parents had that weekend. Thankfully, none of these calls were apparently made to the police, and their home wasn't visited by any blue-uniformed officers. Throughout the weekend, his mother continued to have unpredictable bouts of sobbing, and her husband often had to assist her as she did her best to compose herself.

During one of the telephone conversations, Jeremy could clearly detect excitement and hope in his father's voice. He couldn't hear the exact words but the tone of his voice indicated that what he was told was very good. As soon as he hung up the phone, Mr. Bracken talked excitedly in hushed tones with his wife. Jeremy was able to glean that someone his father worked with told him about a special kind of doctor who was coming to the city. It sounded like this doctor was going to be at the college giving some kind of talk or demonstration.

When Jeremy went to bed, his father sat in a chair in the corner of his bedroom. Even though the police weren't summoned and he hadn't been arrested, Jeremy had the uncomfortable feeling he was a prisoner. During a hushed conversation, Jeremy heard his mother suggest that the gun be locked in the trunk of the car. "I don't want it out of my sight," his father replied. He kept the pistol tucked into the waistband of his slacks the entire weekend. As Jeremy laid in bed, his father was reading the newspaper while leaning back in a chair. Jeremy thought that it seemed like they were in an old cowboy movie and his dad was guarding the criminal in the jail before he was taken out to be hung.

CHAPTER TWELVE

Dr. Ford Freud's Assessment

For quite some time after that, David Bracken kept the pistol with him at all times. He considered a hundred places to hide it but none of them were 100 percent safe. If the old Navy pistol hadn't been a family heirloom, he would have just thrown it into a lake so that no child would ever get his hands on it. But the gun was originally his father's and had been handed down to him, thus he felt obligated to keep it. After the scare with Jeremy, he now looked upon the gun less as a family heirloom and more as something evil. He figured the best way to make sure it never caused injury to anyone was to always keep it close at hand. When he and his wife sat in the university lecture hall, the pistol was tucked uncomfortably into his pants, causing him to shift his position quite a few times during Dr. Freud's lecture. When he and his wife brought Jeremy to the university to be seen by Dr. Freud the day after the lecture, he was still carrying the gun.

As Mr. Bracken drove his wife and son to the university, not a word was spoken. All they told their son was that they were going to meet a special kind of doctor who was visiting from another city. The spring semester was over and the university's campus was fairly quiet. The visiting professor arranged to see the Brackens in one of the psychology department offices. A groundskeeper directed the Brackens to the building that housed the psychology department.

Arts and Sciences Hall was a huge structure that looked like an old towering gothic church. Jeremy was surprised when his father told him that this monolith was only a small part of the school's expansive complex of buildings. This was clearly the biggest school Jeremy had ever seen. There were very few windows and as Jeremy stared up at its façade, he thought the structure would make a good haunted house for Halloween. He wondered if the school turned the building into a haunted house in October as entertainment for its students.

The hallways had high ceilings and marble floors. Their shoes clacked on the floor as they made their way to the psychology department and opened the door. A receptionist greeted them and then took the three of them to an office. All three of them fidgeted nervously and didn't say anything as they waited. Jeremy broke the silence by saying, "This is a really big school." His parents nodded in agreement but said nothing.

Dr. Freud entered the room with a large stack of papers tucked under his left arm. "Mr. and Mrs. Bracken, so nice to see you again," he said, holding out his hand. Both of Jeremy's parents noticed that Dr. Freud was wearing what appeared to be the same dress shirt, tie and sport coat he wore during the previous day's lecture. Mrs. Bracken had a fleeting thought that it looked and smelled like Dr. Freud had likely worn the clothes for several days, but she swiftly pushed it out of her mind so she could focus on the well-being of her son.

"You must be young Master Jeremy," the doctor said, offering his hand to the boy. "Your parents had the good fortune to come to my lecture yesterday and we were able to set up this meeting so that I could talk to you."

"Hi," Jeremy said meekly as he shook the man's hand. Jeremy smelled the pungent odor of tobacco smoke emanating from the man. It was just a typical tobacco smell, not one of the exotic smells that came from Mr. Daymo's cigarettes.

"I am here to help you, Master Jeremy," the doctor explained as he placed the stack of papers on the table and sat down. "My specialized skills are sought out by people all over the world, and today I am here to help you with your problems."

Jeremy didn't say anything. His mother piped in, "Say thank you to the nice doctor, Jeremy."

"Thank you?" Jeremy said softly, in a way that sounded like it was a question.

"Now we have come to the time when I will meet with Jeremy privately," Dr. Freud announced to his parents. "Before I do so, however, it is imperative that the patient realize that I have full and complete authority. Since you and your wife are the child's authority figures, we need to establish with Jeremy that I have the same power, if not superior, as his parents." Mr. and Mrs. Bracken nodded as the doctor explained the process. "To do this, please read aloud to Jeremy what is printed on this paper."

The doctor pulled two pieces of paper from the large stack that he'd brought with him.

"Mrs. Bracken, you will recite the statement first and then Mr. Bracken will follow. Master Jeremy, it is important to this medical process that you listen very carefully to what your parents are about to say to you."

The hand in which Mrs. Bracken was holding the paper was shaking just a little. She cleared her throat and then read from the paper. "It is important that you, state patient's name here...oh, I'm sorry."

"That's okay, it happens all the time," Dr. Freud said. "Please start again, madam."

Mrs. Bracken once again cleared her throat and read from the piece of paper. "It is important that you, Jeremy Bracken, understand and accept that Dr. Ford Freud is here to cure you. Because he is a medical doctor, a psychologist, and a certified public accountant, he has unique skills that no one else has. I, as your parent, hereby demand that you provide complete and true answers to all of his inquiries. When he speaks, you shall treat him as your parent and you will not question him. If you fail to follow his instructions, you will be punished. Do you understand, state patient's name here…I mean, Jeremy?"

Jeremy looked at his parents and said, "Yes?"

His father read the same statement, and then Jeremy's parents were asked to follow Dr. Freud out of the room.

"We will be absent for just a minute, Master Jeremy," the doctor said. "Miss Thompson has been kind enough to stay with you as we make the final preparations."

As Dr. Freud and his parents left the room, the receptionist entered and engaged Jeremy in idle conversation. The Brackens were led to an adjoining room, which had chairs set up facing a glass wall. Through the glass, they could see the receptionist talking to their son. Apparently there was a microphone stashed somewhere in the room, because they could hear the conversation through a small speaker. The Brackens stood in front of the one-way glass and listened as Jeremy told the receptionist about what he planned to do during summer vacation.

"This permits you to see and hear the session without the patient's knowledge," Dr. Freud said, gesturing towards the one-way glass. "A degree of sound can pass from this room into the therapy area, so you will need to remain as quiet as possible during the session." Once the Brackens were seated, the physician left them to observe the proceedings.

The doctor returned to the therapy room and excused the receptionist. After she had closed the door, Dr. Freud sat down at the table opposite of Jeremy. Dr. Freud pulled a long cigar out of the breast pocket of his sport coat and clipped off its ends with a small pocket knife. He lit the cigar with a silver metal lighter and puffed on the cigar until he was sure that the tobacco was lit. Jeremy heard the familiar metal *snap* when the doctor closed the lighter. When the smoke reached Jeremy, he turned up his nose a little at the acrid and awful smell of burned tobacco. Once his cigar was lit, Dr. Freud crossed his right leg over the other and asked, "Why do you think you are having so many dreams? Eh?"

Jeremy felt very small. Even though they were both sitting down, Dr. Freud was a tall and husky man who seemed like a giant to the boy. Jeremy felt like he was a little turtle trying to hide in its shell as a large predator hovered over him. "I don't know," Jeremy said meekly.

Without providing Jeremy any indication that he was going to transition to another topic, Dr. Freud asked, "Why did you steal your father's revolver? Hmm?"

Once again, Jeremy replied, "I don't know."

Dr. Freud held his cigar and pointed the end at Jeremy in a somewhat menacingly gesture. "Did you *not* understand the statements read to you by your parents? You are obligated to be completely truthful with me and provide all of the information that I require. So, let's try this again: why did you steal the gun?"

Jeremy felt the need to defend himself. "I didn't steal it."

"Even if in a truly legal sense there was no theft *per se*, that does not answer the foundational inquiry as to why you stole the gun, does it? What is the answer to that question, Master Jeremy?"

Jeremy thought that the title "Master Jeremy" was odd. The only other person he could remember who called him that was Nasty Nurse. He didn't understand what the word "master" meant in this context. In his mind, "master" meant the guy in control but Jeremy was clearly not in control of *anything* in his life at that point. He wondered if the word was used because the opposite was true, like when Robin Hood called his huge friend "Little John." Whenever the doctor used the phrase "Master Jeremy," Jeremy felt as though what was really being said was *"you idiot."*

"Well, what's the answer, Master Jeremy?" the doctor asked impatiently.

"You keep saying *Master Jeremy*. What do you mean when you say *master*?"

"It's a kind of padlock. I see that you are cleverly trying to avoid my question, Master Jeremy, so I will repeat it. Why did you steal your father's gun?"

Jeremy was confident that saying "I don't know" was likely going to make the doctor mad. In order to hopefully move things along and bring an end to this meeting, Jeremy said, "I thought it looked cool. I guess. Yeah."

"Did you steal the revolver because you were failing to get the amount of attention you desired from your parents?" Dr. Freud suggested.

Jeremy had no idea how to respond, so he was a little relieved when the doctor asked a new question before getting a response to the first one.

"Are you trying to punish your parents for something? Is that why all of these *supposed* dreams and nightmares are occurring, Master Jeremy?"

"No," Jeremy responded. It came out of his mouth sounding squeaky, so he repeated the answer while trying to sound more sure of himself. "No."

"Did you know that sometimes we try to punish our parents even when we are not consciously aware that we are doing so?" Jeremy shook his head. "For example, do you know what hang gliding is?" Jeremy nodded his head. "Did you know that the only true justification for someone to engage in hang gliding is to punish his parents for not letting him play more as a child. Does that make sense?" Jeremy had no idea what the old man was talking about but he decided nevertheless to nod his head in agreement. "A little boy who is trying to punish his parents might tell everyone that he is having dreams and nightmares as a way to get back at his parents. Did you know that?"

The hair on the back of Jeremy's neck stuck out like a porcupine. "I didn't make up *anything*!" he exclaimed. "My dreams are real, *not* made up!"

"Ah," Dr. Freud said calmly without changing the expression on his face, "we have hit a nerve, haven't we, young Master Jeremy? The suggestion that this is all make-believe causes you to become defensive and angry, true?"

Jeremy knew that somehow the doctor was using his tone of voice against him, so he replied in a voice that was as calm as he could make it, "They're real. Not made up."

"Okay, so prove it to me. Tell me about what you see in your dreams." Dr. Freud's voice was now as soft as velvet as he tried to lure his patient to open up to him.

Jeremy looked into the doctor's eyes. "I can't."

"Please," Dr. Freud said soothingly. "Help me prove to your parents that your dreams are not make-believe. You and I can prove it if we work together. What are you so afraid of?"

Jeremy looked at the floor. He could feel the man's eyes on him. "I can't."

"Why not? I'm here to help you prove that you are not making things up."

Jeremy felt like he was on the ropes. No matter what he said, the doctor was adept at turning his words against him. The two sat in silence. Jeremy lifted his eyes and once again met Dr. Freud's. It was clear to Jeremy that the old man was studying everything Jeremy did and everything he said, so Jeremy didn't speak. For a few minutes, neither one of them said anything. Periodically, the old doctor took a puff from his cigar but even when he did so, his eyes didn't stray from his patient's face. The longer the silence went on, the more uncomfortable Jeremy felt. It was as if each passing second of silence caused a vice to be tightened around his chest. Eventually the boy couldn't bear the silence. Jeremy had to say something. *Anything.* He wanted so desperately for the tortured silence to end that he said, "I don't want anything to happen." Jeremy saw Dr. Freud's eyebrows lift.

Still using his kindest and calmest tone of voice, Dr. Freud asked, "Who would cause something to happen?"

The jolt of pain that tore through Jeremy's abdomen was severe. Jeremy wanted to hide the pained expression on his face, so he abruptly turned his head away from the doctor. Jeremy didn't know that he was looking directly into one way glass. In the other room, his parents saw their son's face wrinkle up with pain. They saw his lips part, revealing that his teeth were grinding against each other. Mrs. Bracken's hand went up to her mouth and it was trembling. Mr. Bracken reached over and put his hand on her shoulder.

"Nothing. Nobody. Nothing," Jeremy said between his gritted teeth.

"Are you afraid your father will do something to you? Or your mother?"

Jeremy was incensed and raised his voice. "No!" he yelled.

"A relative? A neighbor?"

Jeremy turned back around and looked into the doctor's eyes. "No," he said resolutely.

"So then, Master Jeremy, *who* is it?"

Jeremy concluded that the best way to survive this interview was to say absolutely nothing. Jeremy crossed his arms and pursed his lips. After sitting in silence for a minute, Dr. Freud asked, "Are you crossing your arms as a symbolic gesture to keep me away from the truth that you are hiding from me?" Jeremy quickly uncrossed his arms and looked at the floor. "Are you now uncrossing your arms because you deep down want to tell me the truth?" Jeremy started to raise his arms to cross them again but decided to just let them hang by his side. When Jeremy refused to answer any questions for awhile, Dr. Freud changed his tact. "You know, Master Jeremy, if you just remain silent, bad things can happen."

Jeremy's eyes shot up and he glared at the doctor. The way the doctor said the phrase *bad things can happen* sounded very much like Mr. Daymo making one of his veiled threats. The measured tone of the doctor's voice was exactly like Mr. Daymo's when he wanted to chastise Jeremy. He looked carefully into the doctor's eyes, wondering if Mr. Daymo's face was going to materialize. As he studied the doctor's face, he noticed that the white portion of the doctor's eyes had a yellowish tinge to it.

"Ah, I see that I have your attention once again," Dr. Freud said, looking into Jeremy's eyes. "You apparently do not wish for *bad* things to happen, do you?" As Jeremy surveyed the doctor's face, he couldn't detect any indication that Dr. Freud was simply another disguise used by Mr. Daymo. The doctor's eyes looked nothing like Mr. Daymo's. "If you help me, Master Jeremy, we can make sure that the bad things do not occur. Does that sound like a good plan?" Jeremy kept staring at the doctor's face but he didn't respond. He still wasn't completely sure that Mr. Daymo might suddenly inhabit the man wearing the tweed sport jacket at any moment.

Dr. Freud tapped his cigar ash into a coffee mug and gave his patient a little time to think in silence. He noticed the small room was filling up with cigar smoke, so the doctor got up from the desk and opened a window. Even as he did this, the doctor kept his young patient in the corner of his eye, looking for any indication that the doctor had broken through the boy's emotional shields. "There, is that a little better?" He sat back down in the chair opposite of his patient and started to follow what he thought might be a promising avenue of inquiry. "What kind of bad things do you want to avoid, Master Jeremy? Hm? Are you afraid of being punished? What if something bad happened to *you*?" The learned doctor was watching his patient's face carefully, but there was no detectable reaction. "What if something bad happened to your best friend?" No reaction. "What if something bad happened to your parents?" The trained eyes of Dr. Freud detected a subtle non-verbal response. The child's pupils constricted just a little when his parents were mentioned. Dr. Freud also saw the muscles in his jaw tighten for a moment. "Would you want something bad to happen to your parents?" The patient shook his head. "Of course not. You want to help them avoid anything bad happening, is that correct?" His patient nodded.

"Good! So let's try to keep bad things from happening. We are united in our wish that bad things not happen to your parents." This declaration did not cause the patient to say anything, so the doctor decided to try another tactic. "How about if we play a little game? Hm? This a fun game called *Back And Forth*." Dr. Freud pulled a few pieces of paper from the stack he brought with him. "It's a lot of fun. I say one word and you say the next thing that comes into your mind. It's a way for us to talk to each other and get to know one another better. It seems like we are wasting a lot of time just sitting here in silence. This game helps act as an icebreaker so we can have a nice chat. Does that sound like fun?" Jeremy didn't respond and kept his eyes on the floor. "So, if I say *dog*, you say...what?"

Jeremy didn't want to play this game, and he still felt his best defense might be to just sit silently and motionless like he was a statue.

When Jeremy didn't respond, Dr. Freud's tone became terser, "You parents commanded you to participate in this session. The same parents who could have something bad happen to them. You can help your parents by talking to me."

Very faintly, Jeremy thought he could hear his mother crying. It sounded like it was coming from the other side of the wall. He turned and looked at the wall but there was nothing there-just a big mirror. The distant sound of his mother's sobbing made Jeremy feel bad. Jeremy felt guilty and embarrassed at the number of tears he'd caused his mother to shed since the dreams had started. How many times had she rushed into his bedroom to hug him after a nightmare? How many times had his mother and father comforted him after something horrible had happened in a dream?

Jeremy turned back to the doctor and replied, "Cat."

Dr. Freud smiled and said, "Good. You are really good at this game."

Jeremy was pretty sure the doctor wasn't being sincere, but he decided not to let it bother him. He nodded at the doctor, indicating that he was ready to continue playing the game. "To truly play this game properly, you have to be completely relaxed while you are playing it. So, I want you to close your eyes, Master Jeremy." Jeremy did as he was instructed. "Good. When you breathe, take slow, long breaths that completely fill your lungs. Now let out that air in four counts: 1, 2, 3 and 4. Four counts in, then four counts out." Dr. Freud's voice became so calm that it was almost hypnotic. "Very good. Again. Now once more. Picture yourself as a feather floating on a breeze." As Jeremy followed the doctor's instructions, he was surprised to feel some of the tension in his neck and shoulders melt away a little. "You are floating. Floating. Letting the breeze guide you. All the while you are taking deep, healing breaths." Now we are going to start the game. Remember, don't think about your answer, just say the word that comes to you, okay?"

"Um hm."

"Tree."

"Leaves."

"Sky."
"Birds."

"Mother," Dr. Freud said, looking closely at Jeremy's face.
"Father."

"Cigar."
"Cigarette."

"Oedipus."
"I don't know what that means."

"Just a one word reply is permitted, Master Jeremy. Just one word. Let's try that again. Remember, only one word replies are acceptable. Oedipus."

"What."

"Oedipus." Dr. Freud said louder.

"What."

"Oedipus." Dr. Freud repeated even louder.

"What. *What* is my answer. *What* is an Oedipus?"

"Oh, I see. Very well, then." Dr. Freud crossed out one of the words on his list and then continued.

"Family."
"Good."

"Vegetables."
"Tomatoes."

"Sun."
"Darkness."

Jeremy was surprised to find that he was kind of enjoying this game. He felt very relaxed and the words came out of him effortlessly.

"Brother."

"Sister."

"Sleep."

"Nightmares."

Dr. Freud jotted a short note on the paper and then said, "Dreams."

"Mr. Daymo, uh, I mean... mowing."

Dr. Freud was confused by Jeremy's reply, and he wasn't sure that he heard the boy's response clearly. He looked up from his notes and asked, "What do you mean when you say *mowing*?"

Jeremy's opened his eyes and they darted around the room as his young mind tried to find something to say that would fix his mistake. "Mowing. Like it's a good day to mow the lawn."

The two sat in silence, staring at each other for a few moments. Dr. Freud shifted in his chair and asked, "So when I said *dreams* the first word that popped into your head was *mowing*?"

"Yeah. Mowing. Is that wrong? Am I winning the game?" Jeremy asked in a trembling voice. Jeremy's imagination was already coming up with a list of horrific and lurid punishments that Mr. Daymo might impose on Jeremy because he uttered his name to the psychiatrist.

"Did you say something more? Did I hear you say that *Mister Day is mowing*?" the doctor asked.

"No!" Jeremy responded quickly and in a volume too high for the small room. "Just mowing." Jeremy coughed a little and then said, "Yeah, mowing." Jeremy tried to shift the focus of the doctor's attention. "So, how many points did I get? Am I winning?"

Dr. Freud took a few moments to jot down some notes and as he did so, he said, "It's not that kind of game, Master Jeremy. It's not a game with winners or losers. It's just a fun game to play."

Jeremy didn't think the game was the least bit fun any longer. After the physician finished jotting down a few notes, he looked back up and Jeremy could feel the old man's eyes burrowing into his head, searching for things that Jeremy had hidden. It was as if the psychiatrist was a peg-legged pirate, digging for treasure in Jeremy's brain which the boy had carefully buried. If Dr. Freud continued to dig and managed to stumble upon Jeremy's treasure chest of secrets, would Mr. Daymo punish him? And punish his parents? Jeremy thought to himself, "I need to be smart. And I need to be strong. I need to be as smart as Bruce Wayne and as strong as Batman. It's just a game. I'm good at games! I can win this game."

Dr. Freud broke eye contact to look down at his list of words, and Jeremy felt an immediate sense of relief. When the doctor was looking down at his papers, it felt less like Jeremy's brain was being surgically dissected by the old man's eyes.

"Let's try a few more, Master Jeremy, shall we? Close your eyes again. Good. More deep breathing. The next word is nighttime."

Jeremy definitely did not say any of the things that first came into his mind: Mr. Daymo; nightmares; scared. Instead, he carefully considered several different responses in his head and tried to decide which one would be the best answer to give.

"You are supposed to say the first thing that comes into your pediatric brain," the doctor instructed. "You are *not* supposed to be thinking about your answers. Now, do as I say and quickly respond to the cue word: nighttime."

Startled a little by the doctor's harsh rebuke, Jeremy blurted, "Tomato." Jeremy wasn't particularly pleased with this response, but it was the only thing that he could think of that wouldn't lead to dangerous follow-up questions about his nightly visitations.

Dr. Freud slammed his pencil down on the table, shattering the lead tip. Jeremy startled and jumped a little in the chair. Dr. Freud raised his voice, "Now you are just being a silly little boy! We are engaging in an important psychological assessment! Do you think this is all a game?"

Jeremy nodded and said, "Well, yeah. *You* told me it was a game."

Dr. Freud closed his eyes and took a moment to inhale a deep healing breath. He absently put his left index finger above his nose in the space between his eyes and massaged it. The psychiatrist tried to compose himself by letting his mind go to his happy place. Oslo, Norway. A gold medallion with the imprint of Alfred Nobel on it. A huge adoring audience.

"Indeed I did. I am fortunate that I have such an attentive patient," the doctor said, but Jeremy didn't think he sounded sincere. Dr. Freud mustered a small grin. "I have another game that we can play, Master Jeremy…" the old doctor said, then quickly corrected himself. "Actually, it's not so much a game as it is an exercise."

"An exercise? Like squat thrusts? I can do lots of those."

For just a moment, the psychiatrist's brain was back in Oslo, basking in the applause of the audience that had gathered for the Nobel Prize ceremony. He said under his breath, "A challenging, chattering child chafes me!"

"Huh?"

Dr. Freud composed himself and once again tried to put a friendly smile on his face in order to put his patient at ease. To Jeremy, the old man only succeeded in making himself look weird and creepy. "Not that kind of exercise. This game…I mean exercise, is called Herman's Picture Exercise. I am going to show you some drawings that are very messy," he said, removing some of the papers from his large stack. "Like this one, for example." He showed

Jeremy a white sheet of paper that had black splotches on it.

"What you need to do is to tell me what you see. Doesn't that sound like fun?" Jeremy didn't reply and continued to watch the doctor suspiciously. It was clear his patient had become sulky and less responsive, so Dr. Freud appealed to the boy's sense of competition. "Aw, come on now, Master Jeremy, are you hesitant to play? It has been my experience that boys are *much* better at this game than girls. All of the boys who have done this have universally done better than girls. Would you like to show me how boys are better at girls when it comes to brain exercises?"

The boy took the bait. Feeling a surge of boyhood pride, he was suddenly more than willing to participate. Jeremy knew that it was a proven fact that boys were better than girls at *everything,* and he was eager to prove it. "Okay, let's do it," Jeremy said with a tinge of excitement in his voice.

"That's very good, young Master Jeremy. I knew you would want to prove that boys are so much more clever than girls," Dr. Freud said with a smirk. He leaned in towards Jeremy and said softly, "We all know that boys can beat girls in *any* kind of task, right?"

"Yeah. Girls are dumb," Jeremy said. "I don't like them."

"What about your mother? She's a girl, would you agree?"

Jeremy considered the question and replied, "Mom's okay. And Grandma. But all the other girls: *ick.*"

The doctor leaned back and jotted a short note. He once again held up the piece of paper towards the boy and said, "So, tell me what you see in this first picture."

Jeremy looked at the splotchy black drawing. It looked like someone had dropped some black paint on paper and then the folded it in half. He remembered in first grade making snowflake pictures in school using a similar process. They dribbled a little green paint on red construction paper and then folded it, creating green paint on red construction paper and then folded it, creating snowflake patterns. When Jeremy carefully considered the black splotch, he thought that it looked a lot like a face. It wasn't a perfectly proportioned face. No, it was an ill-defined and irregular face, with unnatural features. He remembered how he'd seen Mr. Daymo's face materialize many times over the previous months. A dog might be talking to Jeremy and then its muzzle would morph into Mr. Daymo's face. As it did so, the features often looked strange and irregular like the face Jeremy saw on the piece of paper. When he had this thought, a small twinge rippled through his belly. Jeremy didn't need the warning: he wasn't an idiot, for goodness sake! He knew the *last* thing he'd ever say to the old doctor was that this was the face of the other member of the Secret Club.

Jeremy squinted his eyes, trying his best *not* to see Mr. Daymo's face in the splotches. It seemed, however, that the harder he tried to see something other than Mr. Daymo's face, the stronger the resemblance became. He focused his attention intently, trying to see something other than his nightly visitor.

"Come on, Master Jeremy. Just tell me the first thing that comes into your mind. You can do it. Boys are good at this!"

He wasn't sure what the time limit was on giving an answer but he knew that he needed to come up with a response. "A hamburger?" Jeremy said, as if we was not very confident of his response.

The doctor's eyebrows went up and he turned the picture back around so that he was looking at the picture. "A hamburger, you say?" Dr. Freud looked over the top of his glasses and squinted as he examined the inkblot. "Your answer is that *this* is a hamburger?"

Under the stress of the doctor's glare, it was the best answer Jeremy could come up with off the top of his head. In an effort to support the answer, Jeremy pointed to portions of the picture and tried to explain what he saw. "There's kind of like a bun. You can see some meat. Kind of like a hamburger that maybe got dropped on the floor, or something like that." Jeremy didn't think he sounded very convincing. The old man peered at the boy and Jeremy tried to look as though he was being truthful.

After a few moments, Dr. Freud jotted a note on the bottom of the picture and then held up a second inkblot. "What do you see in this picture?"

Jeremy clearly saw that this was a mirrored image of a hand holding a lit cigarette with smoke coming from it. He also knew that the hand holding the cigarette surely belonged to a man wearing a dark businessman's suit. He tried to come up with an answer that was in no way related to what he actually saw but, once again, the more he tried to do so, the more convinced he became that it was indeed what he initially thought it was.

"Answer!" Dr. Freud yelled, which surprised Jeremy and caused him to blurt out what he was thinking.

"I see a hand holding a cigarette, with smoke coming out of it," Jeremy responded truthfully. The boy winced a little, expecting a sharp pain to rip through his belly but there wasn't any. He was sure that Dr. Freud would now pepper him with follow-up questions about who was holding the cigarette and what the smoke smelled like. To Jeremy's surprise and relief, the doctor didn't ask any further questions about the picture. Once again, the doctor wrote a short note on the bottom of the drawing. As he did so, he said in a friendly and supportive voice, "You are very good at this. It seems that boys *are* much better at this game, I mean exercise, than girls." Dr. Freud held up another drawing.

Jeremy jerked backward involuntarily in his chair when he saw the third drawing. His eyes grew large, and his heart started to beat faster. There was no doubt as to what Jeremy was looking at. He saw the unmistakable dark eyes of Mr. Daymo, who had a big sinister grin on his face. Jeremy's eyes darted back and forth between the picture and the doctor, which caused the doctor's white eyebrows to lift with interest.

Jeremy began to wonder if these images were truly random or whether they were *all* drawings associated with Mr. Daymo, deliberately designed to trick Jeremy into telling the doctor about the

Secret Club. But how could this be so? It didn't make any sense! How could anybody know about Dr. Daymo in the first place, let alone know what he looked like? Jeremy looked again at the drawing, and he could almost see Mr. Daymo's face moving as if he was silently laughing at Jeremy's uncomfortable predicament.

"Are you okay, Master Jeremy?" the doctor asked, sounding as if he had some true concern for the boy's wellbeing. "You look pale. What are you seeing in this drawing?"

Jeremy tried to regain his composure, but the more he looked at the face, the more distraught he became. In a flash of insight, he wondered if this meeting with the doctor was just another dream. Was this doctor going to show him pictures of Mr. Daymo until Jeremy finally realized it was actually Mr. Daymo himself seated across from him? He looked at the doctor for any telltale signs that Mr. Daymo's face was about to emerge, but Dr. Freud's face didn't change. Jeremy looked around the room for anything that was out of place, but everything looked normal. The floor was not beginning to melt, and the room did not miraculously change into a forest or a desert.

When he looked back at the drawing, he saw Mr. Daymo's face still grinning at him with satisfaction. Was Mr. Daymo gaining the power to control not only Jeremy when he was sleeping but also his waking world? Were the nightly visits merely the beginning of Jeremy's ordeal? As Mr. Daymo's power grew, would he be with Jeremy all day and all night? Had Mr. Daymo been watching him in the classroom from the hallway? The grinning face on the drawing suggested that this was so. Jeremy put his hands over his face and started to cry. He realized that if Mr. Daymo had become this strong, whatever hope Jeremy had of returning to a normal life was dribbling away.

"What's the matter?" the doctor chastised. He turned the piece of paper around and looked at it carefully. "What are you seeing?

Tell me!" When Jeremy continued to cry and didn't answer, the doctor said in a loud and acidic tone, "What is the problem?"

With his face covered by his hands, Jeremy slowly shook his head and wept. "It's you. I know it's you. Just stop it. I don't want to play anymore."

"Are you saying this is a drawing of me?" Dr. Freud asked. "That is what you see? A picture of me?"

Jeremy nodded as he continued to cry. Mrs. Bracken burst into the room and ran to her son, enveloping him in a hug. Jeremy buried his head into his mother's chest and wept. Jeremy's father was right behind her, and he wrapped his arms around his wife and son.

"Mr. and Mrs. Bracken!" the doctor shouted angrily, jumping to his feet and causing the papers on his lap to fall to the floor. "The session is not finished! You are interrupting us at a critical point in the clinical assessment!" Dr. Freud slammed the hand holding the drawing down on the table to get their attention. None of the Brackens paid any attention to him, however. They were a family of three who, at that moment, were moving as one, rocking back and forth in unison. When it was clear that no further assessment was going to be possible at that point, Dr. Freud threw up his hands in a dramatic gesture of disgust and stomped out of the office.

Later, Jeremy was nursing a cold bottle of Coca-Cola as he sat on a bench in the hallway outside of the psychology department. Behind a closed office door, Dr. Freud was speaking angrily with Mr. and Mrs. Bracken. "We could have been on the brink of discovering something important when the two of you barged into my examination room and destroyed my efforts."

"We're very sorry, doctor," Mr. Bracken said meekly, looking at the floor. "Very sorry. Jeremy just seemed so...so..."

"Did you know that research has shown that providing love and affection to a child is often one of the reasons that pathological pediatric predicaments such as this develop?" The Brackens had their heads bowed as if they were children being punished. "No, of course you didn't know that because you were watching television as opposed to reading scholarly journals!" When he saw the parents' hurt expressions, Dr. Freud was satisfied that he had made them to realize the enormity of their transgression. His fury being satisfied, the doctor cleared his throat and softened his tone. "Despite all that, I am pleased to report that I was able to collect some important data regarding the patient."

Mrs. Bracken raised her head and said, "Please, doctor, tell us what you know."

"Telling you all that I know would take a lifetime, madam. I can, however, explain to you in layman's terms the basics of the process of determining a diagnosis." The Brackens nodded their heads eagerly. "A learned professional with my level of training and experience has the ability to reach presumptive diagnoses based solely on the patient's history. In your son's case, I was able to reach a presumptive diagnosis simply as a result of talking to the two of you on the day of my lecture."

"Really?" Mrs. Bracken said, with amazement and hope in her bloodshot eyes. "Do you already know what my baby's problem is?"

Dr. Freud continued speaking without giving any recognition that she had asked a question. "Once I reach a presumptive diagnosis, it only remains for me to confirm that it is true. This process involves finding data that supports my presumptive diagnosis and dismissing information that does not meet its diagnostic parameters," the doctor explained in a rather pejorative tone of voice. "Once I have found adequate proof that my diagnosis is correct, then we can proceed to administering the predetermined treatment I anticipated. This is the clinical process that is utilized by a specialized professional such as myself who is a true expert and innovator in the field. Luckily for you, I do not need to waste time blindly stumbling around in the dark searching for the cause of the patient's problems. Through copious study, direct experience, and profound clinical acumen, I can diagnose the most difficult of problems before even meeting the patient. I'm sure I don't have to tell you that this is a unique skill that very few have."

Jeremy's father interrupted the doctor, saying, "Again, we're really sorry. It was just that our son was in such..."

Dr. Freud held up his hand, and Mr. Bracken became silent. "I understand all of this is hard for people like you to understand." Dr. Freud's face softened and he chuckled a little bit. "I sometimes forget that to the unwashed masses, the scientific process is very confusing and may even appear to be a magic trick. Despite the fact that I know I have arrived at this patient's diagnosis, the rules of scientific inquiry mandate that I collect some additional data regarding this patient's sleep cycles. I will submit the patient to a sleep study here at the university later tonight. I will arrange to have the requisite monitoring devices brought into this office so that we can study how the patient's body responds while he sleeps."

"Will it hurt him?" Mrs. Bracken asked hesitantly.

"Not at all," Dr. Freud assured. "I will monitor his vital signs and observe his body's movement during sleep. You likely are unaware that there are different levels or cycles of sleep. Dreaming only occurs during the cycle which is characterized by the patient's rapid eye movement, what we refer to as REM sleep."

"His eyes...?" Jeremy's worried mother said.

"You can tell from looking at the eyelids when the patient is in REM sleep. It looks as though something is moving under the eyelids." Dr. Freud closed his eyes and moved them from side to side. The Brackens could see a small amount of movement under the doctor's eyelids. "It is at this time during the sleep cycle that we know that the patient is dreaming. I am particularly interested in the detection of changes in the vital signs and in the involuntary movements of the body during these cycles of REM sleep. Especially since this patient has a troublesome history that includes irregular sleep, frequent nightmares, and the discharging of a firearm, I want his parents to be present for this study. The parents will once again observe the study behind the one-way glass in the adjoining office. I will only agree to complete this analysis if the parents *promise* not to interrupt the sleep study at *any* time."

"We won't. We promise," Mr. Bracken assured the doctor. "We'll stay in the room until you tell us we can come out."

"Very well. Bring the patient to this office at 9:00 PM tonight. We will have all of the equipment set up in this room. The patient will sleep on a gurney as he is monitored by a registered nurse and myself. I will undoubtedly have a number of faculty and graduate students who will want to attend but they will observe the study in the adjacent room along with you, so that we do not make the patient feel more anxious. Please be advised that the room will likely be a little crowded because there are many who have never witnessed a professionally conducted sleep study, and the interest amongst the students and faculty will undoubtedly be high."

"Yes, we understand. If other children can be helped by them watching this study, we're okay with that," Mr. Bracken said.

"It is settled then. No food after 7:00 PM. The soda pop that he is drinking right now needs to be the last caffeine he ingests. At 8:00 PM, give him the pill I am going to provide to you. It is a sedative that will help him fall asleep. Once he enters the sleep cycle, we will be able to probe further for the reasons of this patient's abnormal behavior. I am confident that tonight's study will be very illuminating and provide answers to this pathological behavior."

CHAPTER THIRTEEN

The Sleep Study

Jeremy's parents were wise when they decided not to tell their son about the upcoming sleep study until later that night. They correctly assumed that if they told their son they needed to return to the university later that night, it would cause him even further anxiety. Their son was very quiet and sullen as they left the university. When his parents tried to engage him in conversation about his visit with Dr. Freud, Jeremy quickly changed the subject. In order to raise their son's spirits a little, the three of them went to the zoo. Since it was a cloudy, cool weekday afternoon, there were very few zoo visitors. Gradually, Jeremy's mood brightened as they visited the animals.

He was very excited when his father told him that they were going to have supper at Jeremy's favorite restaurant: Burger Carnival. At supper, his mother gave him a vitamin that wasn't chewable, so Jeremy had to take a big drink of water in order to swallow the pill whole. Jeremy's mood had improved so much as a result of the trip to the zoo and the hamburger supper, his parents felt guilty about taking their son back to the university that night. They knew, however, that even if Dr. Freud didn't have the best bedside manner, he was their best chance to find a cure for their son. They waited until the last possible moment and then explained to Jeremy they needed to have some tests run at the university that night. Jeremy was a little hesitant to go back to the old bearded doctor, but ever since taking the vitamin pill at Burger Carnival, he felt markedly relaxed. Like his parents, Jeremy was deep down still hoping something could be done to help him, so he didn't put up much of a fuss.

Dr. Freud seemed overly friendly when he greeted them. Jeremy was taken to the same room where he and Dr. Freud met earlier that day, but the room looked very different. Now the room resembled a doctor's office examination room. There was a gurney in the middle of the room with several electric monitors and devices surrounding it. Jeremy did a double take because there was a young dark haired nurse in the room who was wearing a white nursing uniform. At first glance, Jeremy thought it might have been Nice Nurse from the hospital, but it turned out not to be so. Much like Nice Nurse, this nurse was very kind and she had deep brown eyes that for some reason instantly caused Jeremy to trust her.

"Tonight we are going to monitor you while you sleep," Dr. Freud said in his most soothing tone. "Nurse Breen and myself will be taking measurements while you sleep." The nurse nodded, smiling at Jeremy who smiled back. "Your parents will be close by in another room. Please say goodnight to them so I can take them to their waiting room."

"I don't have my pajamas," Jeremy said.

Dr. Freud chuckled. "That's okay. We'll just have you take off your shoes and you can lie on this gurney in your regular clothes. Does that sound like fun: sleeping in your clothes?"

Actually, it did sound kind of fun to Jeremy. When he stayed at Rob's house, they usually skipped getting into pajamas and just slept in their clothes. Not wearing pajamas seemed to them to be a little rebellious. His mother and father kissed him and Jeremy was left alone in the room with the nurse.

"None of this will hurt, sweetie pie. No needles or anything like that, so you can relax," the nurse explained to Jeremy. Jeremy was very relieved to receive that information.

Dr. Freud escorted the Brackens to the office with the one way

A CURE FOR NIGHTMARES

glass. With the exception of two empty chairs that had been set up facing the glass wall, it was standing room only in the office. The Brackens were momentarily taken aback at how full the room was. Fifteen or more people were packed into the office to observe the sleep study, most of whom wearing white lab coats. Dr. Freud directed Mr. and Mrs. Bracken to the front row chairs and then took his leave.

After Jeremy laid down on the gurney, he watched closely as the nurse hooked him up to a number of machines. She put cold stickers on his chest, temple, and wrists. "These will just feel a little cold, but nothing bad," she assured him with a smile. Wires protruded from these stickers, which she plugged into machines. Still a little nervous about the proceedings, he laid stiffly on the gurney. Jeremy felt a little like he was some kind of Frankenstein monster, with wires coming from several parts of his body. One of the machines started giving a *beep* noise every time his heart beat and this familiar sound was unexpectantly comforting to him. The *beep* made him think back to the hospital and the pretty nurse with the deep brown eyes. The lights in the room were dimmed and Jeremy stared at the ceiling. *Beep. Beep.*

"Deep breaths for me, Master Jeremy," Dr. Freud said soothingly.

Jeremy was pretty certain that he wouldn't be able to go to sleep. *Beep.* Lying on a gurney while two people watched him was very weird. *Beep.* He wondered how long he'd have to lie there before everyone would just give up. *Beep.* His eyelids felt a little heavy at times, but he was convinced he'd most likely end up staying awake all night. *Beep.*

Jeremy found himself riding his bicycle down a very steep street. There were no cars on the street, and he had the whole road to himself. Although his feet were on the pedals, he wasn't pedaling. The bike was going fast enough on its own just coasting down the big hill that he didn't need to pedal. When he got to the bottom of the hill and started to go up the other side, Jeremy expected the bike to gradually slow down. He was surprised when his bicycle didn't go slower as it went up the hill. Although Jeremy still wasn't pedaling, his bicycle moved up the hill even faster than it had descended.

"I've never gone this fast!" Jeremy thought, feeling a thrill as the air rushed through his hair and whistled in his ears. It was at that moment that he had a sudden revelation: he needed to go very fast because he'd committed a crime. As his bike crested the hill and raced swiftly down the other side, Jeremy remembered that he was running away from the police. He tried to recollect what crime he'd committed. Was it a bank robbery? Yes, it popped into his head that he'd just robbed a bank. Jeremy couldn't remember any of the details of the robbery, just that it had occurred and he was now trying to get away from the crime scene on his bike. He thought, "Where's the money from the bank robbery?" and as if on cue, he heard something fluttering behind him. Still trying to keep an eye on the road in front of him, he carefully twisted his neck to look behind him. He saw that tied to the flimsy metal fender over his rear tire was a large white cloth bag with a big black dollar sign printed on it. Jeremy was concerned to see the bag hadn't been closed tightly at the top and money was flying out of it. The speeding bicycle was leaving a long trail of bills fluttering behind it.

"I've got to go back," Jeremy said, trying unsuccessfully to close up the bag with his left hand as he held onto the handlebars with his right hand. He pushed his feet backwards on the pedals to engage the brakes, but nothing happened. When he got to the top of the next hill and the bicycle was moving even faster, he concluded he'd completely lost control of his bike. Jeremy and his bike were racing down the street, leaving behind them a larger and larger billowing trail of money. Even though he dragged his feet on the pavement, the bike didn't slow down. Despite having two white-knuckled hands on the handlebars, the bicycle wasn't responding, and Jeremy was convinced the bicycle had a mind of its own. He was at the mercy of the bicycle.

The bike suddenly veered to the right and hit a curb, catapulting Jeremy over the handlebars and onto a soft, grassy front yard. He rolled a few times on the lawn and then stopped, sprawled out face-down on the grass. When he looked up, his bicycle was continuing its journey without him but it was no longer leaving a trail of currency behind it. Jeremy got to his feet, planning to backtrack and collect the money that had flown out of the bag during his escape. To his surprise, the long trail of money had vanished. Mouth agape, he looked both directions, but there were no longer any bills fluttering in the air or strewn along the street. There was no wind, so Jeremy couldn't figure out where all of the money could have gone so quickly.

An old man who looked a lot like Dr. Ford Freud walked out of a house and onto a patio. He yelled at Jeremy. "What are you doing in my yard? I didn't say you could be in my yard!" The old man was holding a spatula and brandishing it in a menacing manner as if it was a sword. Jeremy noticed that the man was wearing a white apron that had a cartoon drawing of a big tomato printed on the front of it. The tomato had large cartoon eyes and a menacing look on its tomato face.

Before he could respond to the old man, large hands grabbed Jeremy from behind and pulled his arms behind him. "Got you!" a bellowing voice declared. "You're under arrest, mister!" A police officer in a bright blue uniform held his arms with one large hand and snapped opened a pair of handcuffs with the other. "You're goin' downtown!" the cop bellowed.

As soon as the officer made this statement, Jeremy instantly found himself in a small interrogation room. Jeremy was seated on a metal chair in front of a metal table. He gingerly brought his arms from behind his back and was relieved to see that he was no longer handcuffed. The walls were made of unpainted cement cinder blocks and water was weeping through them as if this was some kind of subterranean dungeon. There was only one door and it looked like it was made out of metal. There was a small opening at the top of the door with three metal bars across it.

Jeremy thought he was in the room alone, so he was startled when there was a voice from behind him. "We've got you now!" Jeremy quickly turned around and saw a different uniformed police officer holding a steaming coffee mug. "You're in a heap of trouble. But you knew that already, didn't you?"

Jeremy shrunk back from the police officer. The room was very small, and the police officer was uncomfortably close to Jeremy. "I am?" the boy said.

The cop walked past Jeremy and over to the metal door, a ribbon of coffee steam coming from his mug. Once he reached the door, he turned around suddenly and glared menacingly at the boy. "Oh, yeah, all kinds of crimes. Robbery. Stealing. Kidnapping. Lighting forest fires. Murder. All of them."

Jeremy searched his memory but he couldn't recall committing any crimes other than the bank robbery, which he recalled very little of at all. He was pretty sure that he hadn't kidnapped someone and was aghast at the mere thought of murder. Jeremy knew for some reason he'd robbed a bank, but he didn't think he'd committed any other crimes. Even if he was willing to admit to the bank robbery, his memory was for some reason devoid of any of the details of that crime. All he recalled was that he somehow robbed a bank and apparently tried to get away on his bike with the bag of loot. "No, you're wrong," Jeremy responded. "I didn't..."

"You did!" the police officer yelled, slamming his fist on the table. "And now you'll have to pay!" Jeremy didn't like the way the cop was glaring down at him. Jeremy wanted to shrink down to the size of a little mouse so he could try to hide from the towering police officer. Although he thought hard about trying to shrink himself, he remained his normal size. "You better tell us everything. And I mean *everything*!"

"I...I..." Jeremy said, trying to respond to the cop. Jeremy had no idea what he was supposed to know that was of such great value to the police department.

"Go ahead. Tell me everything I want to know! There's no reason you shouldn't tell me everything, is there?!"

As Jeremy thought about how to respond to the officer's interrogation, he felt like there was something in his mouth. He wondered if he had knocked out one of his teeth when he was launched off of his bike and landed on the lawn. Carefully, he moved his tongue around inside his mouth, feeling for a dislodged or broken tooth. It was then that he felt more than one thing loose in his mouth. And then he felt movement. "Oh god," he thought, "I knocked out a bunch of teeth!" But that didn't seem right, either.

As the policeman continued to stare at him, Jeremy hesitatingly brought his hand up to his mouth. When he opened his mouth, a large black cockroach scurried out between his lips and onto his hand. Jeremy tried to scream but when he opened his mouth, all that came out was a thick stream of disgusting roaches. He stuck his fingers in his mouth and frantically scooped the wriggling bugs out of his mouth. The sight of the roaches pouring out of his mouth and onto the floor made Jeremy nauseous, and all of the muscles in stomach started to hurt. He continued to put his fingers in his mouth, but there were no more bugs in his mouth. When the bugs hit the floor, they magically turned into Tootsie Rolls, but Jeremy still smashed the wrapped Tootsie Rolls with his shoes as if they were still roaches.

After he stomped on the last one, he heard a metal lighter open and then snap shut. When Jeremy looked up, he saw that Mr. Daymo was wearing the starched blue police officer's uniform and he was smoking a cigarette. A white cloud came from both the coffee mug he held in his left hand and the lit cigarette he held in the other. The smoke from the cigarette quickly filled the small interrogation room with a biting ammonia odor that smelled like the floor wax that his mother used.

Officer Daymo's voice was calm and soothing, like he was telling an infant a bedtime story. "The order I gave you was to keep quiet. You sure were willing to talk to that quack today, weren't you?"

"Quack?" Jeremy asked. "I thought *quack* was what a duck said."

"Quack: it's a word coined during the Black Death. You know, The Plague." Jeremy cocked his head, clearly not understanding the reference. "Never mind. The important thing is that despite my explicit instructions, you seemed more than willing to open your mouth," Officer Daymo said. "I've told you before: talking leads to bad things coming out of boys' mouths. Boys who talk end up letting out secrets. Important secrets."

"No, I tried my best to say nothin'. Really," Jeremy pled to Officer Daymo. "I don't want to get my parents into trouble!"

Officer Daymo looked down at the boy and took a drag from his cigarette. He looked into the boy's eyes with the same intensity that Dr. Freud had used earlier that day. "We've come too far on this journey for our plans to be ruined at the eleventh hour," Officer Daymo said sternly. "How can I make it abundantly clear to you that the next time you talk to that doctor, or anybody for that matter, nothing important should come out of your mouth?" Before Jeremy could promise that he would do his very best, another shower of cockroaches spewed from his mouth.

When he awoke, Jeremy's fingers were in his mouth. He needed to get all of the roaches out of his mouth! As his fingers probed inside of his mouth, however, he felt nothing. There was nothing moving in his mouth except his fingers and his tongue. As soon as he realized that he didn't have bugs crawling around in his mouth, Jeremy was confronted by an old man with a white beard who put his face close to Jeremy's and bellowed in a demanding voice, "What did you dream about, Master Jeremy?" When Jeremy didn't immediately respond, Dr. Freud commanded in an even louder voice, "Tell me now! Before your memory fades! What did you dream about?" The boy was confused to awaken first to the mistaken belief that there were bugs crawling in his mouth and then to be yelled at by the old man. It took Jeremy a moment to realize where he was and that the shouting old man was Dr. Freud.

Dr. Freud yelled again for the boy to tell him what he had just dreamt about. When Jeremy started to say "roaches" a fiercely intense pain shot through his belly and groin, causing him to cry out. Still lying on the gurney, Jeremy's knees were brought to his chin as the pain folded the boy in two. Jeremy grabbed his knees as the searing pain stabbed through his abdomen. Even as Jeremy gritted his teeth through the pain, the doctor kept his face close to his. "What was it? What did you dream about?" the doctor shouted.

The belly pain was so intense that Jeremy felt dizzy. He pushed his fingers into his abdomen in an unsuccessful attempt to release whatever was causing the pain. Based upon how much he hurt, Jeremy was sure that his guts were being curled around themselves like a twist tie. Even when the severe, stabbing pain finally relented and Jeremy caught his breath, the muscles in his abdomen and groin continued to twitch uncomfortably. Jeremy looked up at Dr. Freud, who was towering over him with his arms crossed. "It's gone, isn't it, young man?" the doctor asked with a disgusted tone in his voice. A brief spasm in his belly reminded Jeremy that his answer needed to be a good one, otherwise harm could come to him and his parents. Having no good reply to give, Jeremy just looked at the doctor blankly.

"It's now gone from your short term memory, isn't it?! Now you can't tell me what the dream was about because it is gone from your memory, isn't that right Master Jeremy?"

Jeremy was relieved that the doctor had handed him the perfect, safe response. After he caught his breath, Jeremy said, "Yes… yes… that's what happened. I remembered as soon as I woke up but now I can't remember anymore. I can't remember anything about the dream."

Dr. Freud slapped his thigh with his open hand and turned towards the mirrored wall. "Just as I suspected! As we know, dreams are typically only kept in the memory of the patient for a short time. If the memory is not adequately processed and placed into long term memory, the recollection of the dream is lost. That is why I asked the patient to tell me about the dream as soon as he awoke." The doctor made this declaration as he faced the wall, so Jeremy wasn't sure who he was addressing. "You might as well come into the room, Mr. and Mrs. Bracken: I have collected all the data that is available."

Jeremy's mother and father came into the office and hugged their son. His mother stroked his hair, which was a little sweaty along his temples.

"There is nothing more to do," Dr. Freud said, then waved his hand dismissively towards the Brackens. The old doctor started to collect his papers, mumbling as he stuffed them into his tattered leather briefcase. While Dr. Freud was preoccupied with the paperwork, the nurse asked the parents about Jeremy's abdominal pain. They told the nurse of Jeremy's bowel obstruction and that he had undergone abdominal surgery in November.

Dr. Freud had already stomped out of the room when the nurse called out to him. "Dr. Freud?"

He returned to the doorway and replied tersely, "What is it now, nurse?"

She hurriedly moved to the doorway and said something under her breath to the old doctor. One of his eyebrows lifted.

"Mr. and Mrs. Bracken," the doctor said, "tell me about your son's abdominal pain." The doctor walked back into the room and the Brackens repeated the story they had just shared with the nurse.

It was nearly 2:00 AM when the Brackens were released to go home. Before they left Arts & Sciences Hall, Jeremy's parents were instructed by Dr. Freud to return to the university later that morning so that they could discuss the results of the sleep study and the physician's conclusions.

Once they got home, Jeremy fell asleep very easily. It seemed the effects of the hamburger supper were lingering, because he still felt sleepy and relaxed. He dreamt he was sitting on the witness stand in an immense courtroom. The judge had three heads and each of them was asking questions of Jeremy at the same time. When Jeremy tried to speak, he found that his mouth wouldn't open. When he raised his fingers to his lips, he discovered his mouth had been sewn tightly shut. Jeremy's fingertips felt where the thick sewing thread dove into his lips and then back out. As Jeremy wondered how he was ever going to eat or drink with a mouth that was sewn shut, he was awakened by his mother's gentle rubbing of his shoulder.

"Time to get up, honey," she said with a worried smile. "We need to go back to the school to talk to the doctor one more time."

* * *

Dr. Freud was talking to a colleague in the hallway outside of the psychology department when the Brackens arrived. "If it's okay with you, Master Jeremy, I'd like to talk to your parents alone in the office," Dr. Freud said. "I know you like soda pop and comic books, so I have procured the necessary means of helping you pass the time." Dr. Freud gestured towards the large church pew in the hallway, which had a can of Orange Crush and an Archie comic book sitting on it.

Jeremy was still tired and a little groggy, so he silently took a seat once again on the wooden bench. He thought, "Orange Crush and Archie? Did he think that I was a girl?"

Dr. Freud reached into the pocket of his weathered sport coat and pulled out a piece of candy. "The vending machine did not have any candy bars. Would you like a Tootsie Roll?" Jeremy looked at the piece of candy held by the doctor and recoiled, shaking his head violently. "Okay, have it your way," the doctor said, unwrapping the Tootsie Roll and popping it into his mouth.

When Jeremy was out of earshot, Mrs. Bracken told the professor that she was hesitant to leave her son alone in the hallway, as he still seemed a little shaken. Dr. Freud advised her they needed to have a candid conversation outside of the child's hearing and that Jeremy would be just fine.

Dr. Freud opened the door to the office from where Mr. and Mrs. Bracken had watched the testing of their son. Jeremy's parents were surprised to see that the room was once again full of people. Seeing the parents' hesitation, Dr. Freud said, "I trust that including these colleagues in our debriefing will be acceptable to you?" Dr. Freud turned his back towards the Brackens without waiting for a reply. The doctor walked across the room and seated himself in the tall leather chair behind dark wood desk. Dr. Freud gestured towards the two empty chairs in front of the desk. "Please take a seat, Mr. and Mrs. Bracken, and we will discuss my findings." Jeremy's parents sat in the chairs as the gathered dignitaries stood nearby and silently watched.

Dr. Freud leaned back in the desk chair and appeared relaxed as he began to discuss his evaluation of the case. "As I explained to you, my abilities empower me to reach a presumptive diagnosis based solely on key facts related to the patient's history. This is a skill that very few medical clinicians have, but when it is applied by a trained practitioner of the medical and psychological arts, it is very effective. Whereas a lesser experienced physician would require months of investigation and therapy in order to root out the cause of a patient's problem, I am able to reach a diagnosis with speed and accuracy. This economy of action is of great benefit to everyone involved. The patient is diagnosed swiftly and appropriate treatment can be instigated without delay. The patient's family is rewarded by the doctor's swift skills because they now have a definite diagnosis. In addition, the practitioner is now free to provide services to additional patients, as opposed to spending his time wallowing in doubt."

The Brackens noticed that some of the people in the room were nodding their heads. Mrs. Bracken had a handkerchief in her hand and she was squeezing it tightly. Mr. Bracken noticed the muscles in his wife's fist tensed each time she squeezed the handkerchief. He could also see the toll that the strain had taken on his wife's lovely face. He placed his hand lovingly on hers, and she managed to smile just a little at her husband. The two of them were pulsing with several emotions all at the same time. Anticipation. Fear. Concern. Hope.

Dr. Freud crossed one leg over the other. He leaned his head back and turned his face upward towards the ceiling, as if he was contemplating a difficult chess move. "In Master Jeremy's case, I gathered a great deal of information during my short initial visit with the parents on the evening of my lecture." Dr. Freud brought his hands together and raised them to his chin as he thought about the conversation. "The parents shared with me that Jeremy had been having increasingly vivid and disturbing nightmares. Each morning, the patient reported he could not remember the subject matter of any of these dreams." The Brackens nodded in agreement. "The fact the patient often spoke and even screamed in his sleep as well as the presence of physical manifestations, such as extreme sweating, elevated my concern that the psychologic phenomena called night terrors may be involved. The patient's parents were often roused from their slumber due to the patient's outbursts, and the parents responded by providing emotional support and comfort. The event that brought the parents to me was one in which Jeremy stole a gun from his father and fired it in his bedroom."

"I don't know if he actually *stole* the gun..." Mr. Bracken began but quickly became silent when the doctor raised his right hand.

"He secretly took a gun from the parental bedroom. He *stole* the gun. When he was confronted by his parents, the patient reported, not surprisingly, that the theft of the gun was related to his vivid nightmares." Dr. Freud smiled a little and chuckled as he said under his breath, "Of *course* he said that."

"Huh?" Mr. Bracken asked, turning his head so that his right ear was closer to the doctor.

"Nothing, just a comment to myself," the doctor said, lowering his head and smiling at the Brackens. He raised the tips of his fingers to the fold in his forehead between his eyes, making himself look like a pious monk who was praying. Dr. Freud closed his eyes and continued, "This information, added with my training and experience in this field, was enough for me to reach a presumptive diagnosis. In fact, I was quite sure that I had reached the correct diagnosis with no input from the patient himself. It was what I believe a golfer might refer to as a *hole-in-one!*" Dr. Freud smiled and made a mental note that he should use this clever metaphor in one of his future publications.

"Yes, I had it figured out." Dr. Freud opened his eyes and pulled his chair close to the desk so that he was looking directly at Jeremy's parents. His facial expression changed. Dr. Freud looked very stern and he almost appeared that he had abruptly become angry. "But my presumptive diagnosis turned out to be...erroneous! Yes, you heard me right: *I*, Dr. Ford Freud, Professor of Psychology and Medicine, was wrong!" A few of the gathered throng gasped.

Dr. Freud sat back in his chair and his expression softened. "You see, in my trained mind, I painted a picture of what characteristics I expected the patient to possess. I believed I would meet a very extroverted, creative child. The reason for this presumption is that difficulties with vivid or disturbing dreams often develop in very creative and socially detached children. They find the real world to be mundane, so they create their own fantasy world full of wonderment and excitement where they can live out extraordinary lives as if they were Peter Pan." The doctor waved his hand dramatically like it was holding a magic wand. "Unfortunately, these are the patients who typically engage in mind-altering drugs, beginning with alcohol and then proceeding to illegal psychedelic substances."

What Mr. and Mrs. Bracken both heard was that their son was destined to become a drug addict, and their faces drooped with disappointment and heartbreak.

"With your permission, I spoke with the patient's teacher over the phone prior to my first meeting with the patient. His teacher described him as a fairly good student but commented further that he was not particularly creative or imaginative. This description was *not* what I expected to hear. The patient she described was *not* Peter Pan. A lesser professional would have become stumped at this point, but I was not. Although I was surprised she did not describe an inventive and imaginative child, I was undaunted.

"Through the scientific and methodical process of accepting the things that supported my diagnosis and questioning any data that was unsupportive, I remained confident I had found the reason for his aberrant behavior. I anticipated that who I was going to meet was indeed going to be Peter Pan." Dr. Freud paused for effect, making sure that he had the complete attention of the parents and the gallery. When the moment was right, he exclaimed, "But I did NOT meet Peter Pan!" He once again dramatically waved his magic wand. Despite his admission of error, the doctor had a wide, beaming grin on his face. "The human mind is so complex that it can mislead even a renowned expert!"

For some reason, Mr. and Mrs. Bracken felt that the loud and jolly statement by the doctor was in some way good news for their son. They remained rapt with attention, hoping the learned doctor would soon tell them that their son was *not* destined to be a drug addict.

"Yesterday I met a child that was *not* Peter Pan. To the contrary, during our interview, this patient revealed that he was a very *uncreative* and *unimaginative* child. His responses to my testing revealed that he was not the gifted free-spirit that I had anticipated. Instead, he revealed himself as being rather dull and unimaginative." Mr. Bracken shifted forward in his chair and opened his mouth to object to this characterization of his son, but Dr. Freud held up his hand before he could speak. "I mean this in the cold, detached and professional sense of the word. This is not, I can assure you, intended to be an indictment of the patient or on how he was raised by his parents." Mr. Bracken still felt the need to speak in defense of his son, but the doctor's hand remained raised and he decided he had no other choice but to settle back in his chair and remain silent.

"His responses to the Word Association Test and the Rorschach Test were very mundane. For instance, consider his response to this picture." Dr. Freud showed the parents and the dignitaries one of the Rorschach inkblots.

"In response to Panel 1A, the patient reported to me that he saw...a hamburger." A couple of the gathered faculty members snickered under their breath. Dr. Freud laced his fingers together and put his hands on the desk. "It became clear to me that this was *not* a gifted child who was trying to escape an uninteresting mundane world in order to frolic in his own exciting alternative world. As the clinician, I was facing a logical conundrum. I anticipated that I would be speaking to a whimsical Peter Pan, but instead I was speaking to an unimaginative Ralph Kramden." One of the faculty members standing in the back of the room tittered a little. "As you know, I continued to make inquiries of the patient during our interview in order to discover why this paradox existed. I felt I was close to revealing what was being hidden from me during the latter stage of the Rorschach test. Unfortunately, that was when you, Mrs. Bracken, barged into the room and broke the analytic interface between the patient and me."

"Again, we're really sorry..." Mr. Bracken said but stopped when the doctor again raised his hand for silence.

"During the time interval between the initial patient meeting and your return last night for the sleep study, I pondered this case. There was data that seemingly did not support my initial diagnosis and this was, of course, very distressing to me. I re-evaluated all of the information again and moved the puzzle pieces into alternate positions. After much deliberation, I concluded that the likely explanation for this patient's aberrant behavior was that this patient was acting out in order to get attention from his parents and especially from his mother. Often time, he cried out in distress in the middle of the night and his parents responded promptly. The parents' response to the dreams acted as a positive reinforcement for the patient's behavior. When his vivid dreams and nightmares over time failed to elicit the response he was craving, he went so far to steal a gun in order to shock his parents into paying attention to him."

Mrs. Bracken quietly began to sob. She felt the doctor was explaining to them how they had failed as parents. Her husband put his hand on her shoulder and squeezed it gently in an effort to give her strength.

"Ahhhh," Dr. Freud said, smiling and holding up an index finger, "but there was one more unexpected twist in this case. Once again, the human mind tried to fool me but I was too clever for it!" A little bit of hope returned to the hearts of Jeremy's parents. They both wished that the doctor would just tell them the final conclusions he had reached but they continued to remain silent and waited as patiently as they could. "Sadly, the sleep study itself provided no helpful information. The patient's vital signs, physical reactions and periods of REM sleep were all normal and typical. I was about to leave the room, believing that the answer to the patient's behavior was simply a child's desire to get parental attention. There was something very subtle, though, that seemed to be in play. In the midst of this very complicated clinical picture, there was a variable that was trying to hide from me. I was determined not to give up until I found that missing piece. Before ending the session, I decided to explore one last avenue of inquiry.

"You will remember that when the patient awoke, he complained of intense abdominal pain. I instantly recognized that this was a new variable to be considered in the overall analysis. Previously, neither the patient nor his parents told me of the patient's bowel surgery. This ended up being the subtle and unlikely key that unlocked the solution to this puzzle. As it turns out, all of the dreams and nightmares were not merely a mundane and unimaginative means of getting attention from his parents. It was something much more...primal."

Mr. and Mrs. Bracken could hear the gathered guests' pencils furiously scratching notes on their notepads. It felt to Mr. Bracken that the energy level in the room had increased as everyone anxiously awaited to hear Dr. Freud's ultimate conclusion.

"Last year, the patient developed a bowel obstruction that became strangulated, thus interrupting the blood supply to the bowel. A successful bowel surgery was performed whereby the area of obstructed bowel was removed and the two ends were reconnected. His post-surgical recovery was uneventful.

"However, the patient periodically had instances of intense pain in his abdomen and upper groin. As you may or may not know, after a surgery of this type, the body creates scar tissue. This reparative tissue can become hard and inflexible. If the scar tissue limits the movement of the surrounding structures, in this case the bowel, we refer to these restrictive growths as adhesions. This sturdy scar tissue can cause problems for any post-operative patients but bowel surgery patients are at particular risk. The scar tissue and adhesions can interfere with the normal movement of the bowel," the doctor held out his hand horizontally and made the motion of a waves on a body of water, "and this restrictions can cause pain. The bowel is very mobile and it can become obstructed due to the adhesions impeding its normal movement.

"The field of physiological psychology is a fascinating one in which we study how a physical event can cause a change in patient behavior. For example, if a child is bitten by a dog, he will likely experience a series of psychological phenomena in future dealings with canines: typically anxiety and apprehension. When such a child is approached by a dog, we can also see a physiologic reaction such as an increased heart rate, faster breathing, and sweating.

"In this case, I was able to conclude that the patient's vivid dreams and sleep disturbances were brought about as a result of the underlying small bowel problems. The emergency bowel surgery was certainly a very traumatic event in this patient's young life. In addition to the ordeal of the emergency surgery, the patient continued to experience painful abdominal symptoms after returning home. These significant episodes shocked the patient's young brain, which led to the development of the abnormal and pathological psychological phenomena classified as night terrors. His disruptive dreams and nightmares are a psychological manifestation of the underlying somatic, or physical condition. We have here an instance where a seemingly unrelated event, the bowel surgery, was the cause of all of the young patient's aberrant psychological problems."

"Then, why the gun?" Mr. Bracken asked, unconsciously touching the pistol that he still kept tucked into his belt and covered by his shirt.

"Yes, the gun," Dr. Freud said, smiling broadly. As the doctor prepared for this presentation, he anticipated that one of the gathered dignitaries would surely ask about the patient's use of the weapon. The professor had gone so far as to rehearsing an informative and scholarly response to this inquiry. He looked at the Brackens and said, "I am quite sure that neither of you are familiar with the scientific idiom called Ockham's Razor." While Mr. and Mrs. Bracken shook their heads, the faculty members and graduate students nodded with recognition. "Dr. Ockham posited that you should not look for more than one cause when a single cause can explain the behavior. Ockham's Razor is often referred to as the

Rule of Parsimony. As I have written and said…"

As Dr. Freud continued to speak, Mrs. Bracken leaned over to her husband and whispered in his ear, "What is parsimony?"

Mr. Bracken whispered in her ear, "I thought it was a garnish."

Mrs. Bracken said, "Ah" and nodded as if she understood the reference. Mr. Bracken, nodded as well, and made a mental note to ask his wife how a little piece of green sprout made any sense in this discussion.

"…several times, however, Dr. Ockham is *not* a god and he is often wrong. It has been my experience that Ockham's Razor is often used by lazy practitioners who find one cause for the problem and then decide to stop searching. In this case, the use of the gun does not fit with the explanation that this patient's actions are guided by his post-operative pain. We can all agree that the gun has seemingly no relation to the pain. It is totally unrelated and sticks out like the proverbial sore thumb. The reason for this, however, is quite simple. For this patient, Ockham's Razor fails. It fails because human beings are more complex than Dr. Ockham would have us believe.

"The gun is a manifestation of underlying unacceptable non-conformist behavior. The fact that the patient has behavior brought about by the surgical pain does not change the fact that the patient had pre-existing anti-social tendencies. Take, for example, his decision to gorge himself on Halloween candy. While this seems like a harmless example of a child's innocent overindulgence, we can see now that this was the genesis of a pattern of non-conformist behavior. As the patient ages, we can anticipate a greater number of such actions occurring and the severity should increase. The theft of the gun, I have discovered, is the result of a second independent psychological phenomena in this patient. The post-operative pain and eccentric dreaming surely accelerated the patient's underlying non-conformist tendencies."

The crowd murmured and Dr. Freud's satisfied smile became larger. "Ockham has failed us once again because the post-operative pain alone does not explain the use of the weapon. One explanation does not answer all of the questions posed by this difficult case study. It takes an expert such as myself to have the courage to turn his back on Dr. Ockham and resolutely search for the deeper answers that are hidden from us."

Dr. Freud paused and looked over his small audience for dramatic effect. Once he was assured that everyone's attention was baited, he summarized his findings with a flourish, "The enigma of this patient's bowel-bred bizarre behavior has been broken! This proves again that the patient's brain will try to fool you, but you have to be smarter than the pathological brain!"

Applause erupted from those who had gathered in the room. Mr. Bracken clapped his hands a couple of times but wasn't completely sure why everyone was so enthusiastic.

In the hallway outside of the main door to the psychology department, Jeremy sat quietly on the bench. He wasn't interested in the can of soda pop or the Archie comic, so they both sat unopened on the bench beside him. To cut down on utility expenses, most of the lights were turned off during the summer, which left the main hallway grim and shadowy.

From the moment he sat down on the bench and his parents went into the psychology department, Jeremy eagerly listened for the sound of his parents' return. There wasn't much traffic in the hallway. A few men wearing business suits nodded at Jeremy as they passed him and went into the psychology department. A secretary came out of one of the other doors and asked Jeremy if he needed anything. Jeremy said no, and the woman click-clacked down the hallway.

He frequently squirmed uneasily on the wooden bench, as it was hard and uncomfortable. As the minutes passed, Jeremy was both excited and apprehensive, still holding out hope that the old doctor and the other adults could find a way to help him out of his predicament. All of Jeremy's schemes had failed, and he didn't think that he'd be able to come up with any other ways to solve the problem. When he heard some distant applause coming from the psychology department, Jeremy thought this might be a good sign for him. Hopefully.

After the applause in the room had quieted, Mrs. Bracken asked in a very meek voice, "But...but what do we need to do for Jeremy? What about my son?"

Dr. Freud held up his hands to quiet the crowd. "Yes, of course. The patient's mother has brought up the issue of treatment and rightly so. Now that I know the cause of the patient's eccentric dreaming, I can easily prescribe a cure. While we have no way to control the process of scar tissue development and we cannot eliminate the chances of future discomfort caused by bowel adhesions, we can disrupt the line of communication between the body and the brain. To break the lines of communication, I shall prescribe a nightly dose of a Dopamine-based medication. This medication will change the chemical balance in the brain by inhibiting certain neurotransmitters and their receptors. What this drug in particular is designed to do is to create a level of disassociation in the brain. In other words, we are interfering with the mode of communication between the brain and the body. In addition, we are interfering with the brain's internal communications, thus achieving a break in the link between the pain the patient has in his abdominal area and the response by the sympathetic nervous system."

"Sympathetic?" Mr. Bracken said.

"Sympathetic. It means compassionate." There were a couple titters from the back of the room. "This will keep both the typical and atypical post-operative pain from interfering with the patient's sleep. By interrupting this line of communication, the unconscious brain will be able to function independently of the ongoing pain. As a result of this disassociation between the physical and mental processes, the patient's difficulties with dreams and nightmares will be mitigated if not extinguished altogether." Once again, polite applause filled in the small office.

Up until this point, the people in the room had tried to remain quiet and respectful of the Brackens. However, it was now as if the room had become the site of a press conference, as the assembled dignitaries began to inundate Dr. Freud with follow up questions, seeking further details about how he was able to successfully diagnose this patient. The questions asked and the answers given were filled with complicated technical terms that had no meaning to the Brackens. The acerbic dialogue between the doctor and his contemporaries meant very little to Jeremy's parents, and they were left to look at each other with confused faces. After fifteen minutes of detailed and complicated questions and answers, the people in the room again applauded and then started to disperse.

Dr. Freud shook the hands of his patient's parents and gave them a handwritten prescription slip. "The patient should take this elixir once per night, 60 minutes before bedtime. I would be most grateful if you would call me in a month to report how the patient is doing. Here is my card. The phone number will be long distance but I will accept your collect call."

The dean of the psychology department announced that there would be a short celebration in the faculty lounge before Dr. Freud left for the airport. Mr. and Mrs. Bracken had plenty of follow up questions of their own to ask the doctor, but he was quickly engulfed by important men who were talking to him excitedly. As Dr. Freud spoke with these professional people, the entire throng moved as a group towards the faculty lounge.

When smiling and talkative adults began streaming out of the office, Jeremy studied their faces. If there was no hope for him, he figured that the people would be sad and sullen. Dr. Freud came out of the office, surrounded by a pack of enthralled followers who were peppering him excitedly with questions and accolades. It was as if Dr. Freud had just scored the winning touchdown at the university's homecoming game and he was swarmed by adoring fans. Neither the doctor nor his entourage paid any attention to Jeremy as they passed him in the hallway.

Jeremy thought that it was a good sign that the throng of adults appeared to be very animated and happy with what they had just heard Dr. Freud say. Surely this was proof that the doctor had figured it all out, Jeremy thought. The only adults who came out of the office who were not smiling were the two adults that were the last to exit: his parents. They still had the same concerned looks on their faces they had when they entered the room. When she saw her son, his mom flashed Jeremy the strained and uncomfortable smile Jeremy had become accustomed to seeing. She looked as though she was trying her best to look happy but what it looked like to Jeremy was she was gritting her teeth as she was undergoing an invasive dental procedure.

"Okay, hon," she said, trying to sound carefree, "now we get to go home!"

"We need to stop at the drug store first," his father announced, "and then we can go home and have some lunch. Sound like a good idea?"

"Sure," Jeremy said unenthusiastically, carefully studying his parents' faces. When their faces did not provide any clues as to what happened, Jeremy asked, "What did the doctor say?"

His parents looked at each other for a moment and his dad said, "He said things look good. All the tests you had done last night were normal. That's good news, isn't it?! All in all, he said everything looks good, son!" Jeremy didn't show the relief or happiness on his face his father had expected to see, so he added, "The doctor gave us a little bit of medicine to take at night time and things should get lots better, sport."

As they walked to the car, Jeremy continued to carefully watch and listen to his parents. He wasn't at all convinced they had provided him the whole story. While they travelled back to the house, he tried to snare any tidbits of additional information. From the backseat of the car, he listened carefully to what his parents said and how they said it. His eight-year-old brain, however, wasn't able to detect the truths shrouded within the subtle communications between his parents. Jeremy failed to notice the undercurrent of concern and apprehension in their voices. Jeremy noticed, however, that everything his parents said and did for the rest of that day seemed to be somehow stilted and orchestrated. The trip to the drug store, his mother making lunch and the three of them playing Monopoly afterwards all seemed to be a scripted television show in which Jeremy was just one of the characters. It seemed to the boy that what was occurring in his world had all been predetermined and he was just along for the ride.

After supper that evening, his mother told Jeremy he needed to take the new medicine prescribed by Dr. Freud. When she advised Jeremy of this, he noticed that her voice was tentative. Typically, when his mother told him he needed to take a medicine, she did so with a confident and all-knowing voice.

"You need to take this so you don't cough so much," his mother would state firmly.

When she told him that night that it was time to take the new medicine, her voice sounded shaky and uncertain. She poured a thick red liquid from the bottle into a tablespoon and encouraged to Jeremy to swallow it quickly. He was able to do so, even though it seemed to be as thick as turkey gravy and tasted like old tires. The aftertaste was awful and he almost gagged, as it felt like the thick liquid got stuck in the back of his throat. Luckily, his mother

A CURE FOR NIGHTMARES

had already poured a glass of juice and he chased the foul tasting medicine with cool, sweet tomato juice. When the medicine finally slid down inside him, Jeremy felt almost instant warmth spread down into his stomach.

It didn't take long for Jeremy to start feeling strange, like he had fluttering butterflies throughout his body. Sometimes the fluttering sensation was so strong he scratched at his skin. As they watched television together while snuggled on the couch, Jeremy found it increasingly difficult to concentrate.

"I feel a little funny," Jeremy said, rubbing his right temple. He noticed a pensive look exchanged between his parents.

"Probably just the new medicine," his mother soothed, putting his head on her chest and stroking his hair.

After watching television a little while longer, Jeremy said, "If it's okay, I think I'll go to bed. I think I'm tired." Jeremy rubbed his eyes. "I think I'm tired. Yeah," he said in a detached tone.

After brushing his teeth, Jeremy lay in his bed, looking up at the ceiling. His mother had closed the door most of the way but kept it open just a crack. Although the hallway and bedroom were dark, he had the distinct feeling that his mother and possibly his father were watching him through the small opening. Just in case they were watching him, he said, "I'm okay. Don't worry about me. I'm okay. Honest injun."

Although he felt relaxed and sleepy, it took him longer to fall asleep than he'd expected. Whenever he was about to doze off, the fluttering sensation that was travelling through his body roused him. Even after he eventually fell asleep, the sensation of butterflies flapping their wings inside of his body continued. As he dreamt, he still felt that funny fluttering sensation throughout his body.

CHAPTER FOURTEEN

The Maestro

Cold air nipped at Jeremy's nose. He was sitting next to Santa Claus on his sleigh and they were soaring through the crisp winter air. The fluffy brown and white tails of the reindeers pulling the sleigh were moving in unison to the left and then to the right. The jingling of sleigh bells was unusually loud, as if someone was shaking them right next to Jeremy's ears. They were so loud that Jeremy swatted around his ears with his mittened hands but he felt nothing. To Jeremy's left sat the larger-than-life St. Nicholas, with a bulbous red nose and lots of white whiskers covering his face. Santa looked down at the boy and nodded, bellowing out his trademark laugh. In the back of a sled was a huge cloth bag teeming with wrapped presents. A few of the presents spilled out of the bag and rocketed downward as if they were guided missiles. Jeremy watched as each of the errant packages zipped down into chimneys. The sleigh descended onto a snow covered roof and slid to a stop. Santa jumped from the sleigh and pulled an empty bag from his belt.

As he joyfully laughed "Ho, ho, ho!" he fished out some packages from the back of the sleigh and put them into the smaller bag. "Let's go, Santa's little helper!" he said and marched resolutely towards the chimney.

The roof was steeply sloped and covered with snow, so Jeremy was hesitant to get out of the sleigh. From his vantage point, he wasn't sure how it was that the sleigh and its reindeer were able to remain securely on the precariously steep rooftop. Jeremy looked down and felt a little dizzy when he saw how high up he was. His mittens grabbed onto the side of the sleigh and Jeremy decided that staying in the sleigh was the safest option.

From the chimney, Santa gestured towards the boy and said, "Come on, Jeremy. We have a lot of visits to make tonight!" In a flash, Jeremy was no longer in the sleigh. Instead, he found himself standing next to Santa on the chimney. Before Jeremy could figure out how he got there, he and St. Nick were sucked into the chimney and deposited into a living room.

"Wh...what?" Jeremy stammered as he tried to get his bearings.

Santa leaned down to Jeremy and put a white gloved finger to his lips, "Shhhh."

Santa tiptoed around the room in an exaggerated and cartoon-like manner, which caused Jeremy to think of how the Grinch did so on the cartoon. After waving his hand over the stockings nailed to the mantel, candy canes and toys suddenly filled them. Still tiptoeing, Santa went to a small table next to the hearth and took a bite out of a cookie that had been left for him to sample. He nodded with satisfaction and then tiptoed down the hall, gesturing for Jeremy to follow him. Jeremy didn't want to move. He felt like an invader or a burglar and looked around to see if he could escape. Once again, however, Jeremy was instantly transported to Santa's side.

The large man in the red and white furry suit tiptoed into one of the bedrooms. Lying in bed was a little girl with pigtails and a long candy cane held in her hands. Although this was a *real* girl and not a cartoon, Jeremy somehow knew she was Cindy Lou Who from *The Grinch Who Stole Christmas*. Santa once again gestured for Jeremy to be quiet, and Jeremy once again looked for a way to get out. When St. Nicholas grabbed Jeremy's hand, the two of them were sucked into the girl's head in the same manner that they had been pulled down into the chimney.

Santa Claus and Jeremy were surrounded by a swirling vortex of colorful lights. Bright explosions of color filled the sky and the ground undulated as if they were standing on a water bed. Sounds, lights, colors, and voices accosted Jeremy's senses. He wanted to close his eyes and cover his ears but he could do neither for some reason. Santa Claus faded away and was replaced by a man wearing a black tuxedo with tails. The man raised his arms, and the cacophony of sights and sounds softened and quieted. In front of the man a podium appeared, which he tapped with the baton he held with the thumb and forefinger of his left hand. The tapping sound that came from the podium was thunderous and amplified, as if the tapping had been made by Thor's hammer.

All of the colors and sounds froze, seemingly in response to the conductor's command. Slowly and methodically, the man waved his hands in the air. Jagged horizontal lines took shape, looking like what Jeremy had seen on television when the reception was poor. Trees, hills, valleys, and grass eventually took form. Initially, they looked crude and a little cartoon-like. Over time, everything became as clear as a photograph. Soon Jeremy and the man in the tuxedo were standing in a beautiful meadow. Jeremy thought this was what he would see in his mind if he pictured a perfect countryside scene. There were miles of rolling green hills dotted with lush adult trees and in the distance was a farm with a big red barn.

As he surveyed the area, Jeremy saw the sleeping girl lying under a shade tree. She opened her eyes and initially seemed to be unsure of where she was. After she stood up and looked around, she giggled. Galloping over the hill was a purple horse with a yellow tail that sparkled. It stopped under the tree and nuzzled the girl. Cindy Lou Who held out her arms as if she wanted to be picked up, and she was grabbed by unseen hands. After she was placed on the back of the horse, it resumed its galloping with the girl astride. Both the little girl and the horse were gaily laughing as they disappeared over the hill towards the farm. The entire scene disappeared, as if it had all been drawn on an Etch-A-Sketch that had now been turned upside down and shaken.

Jeremy was back on the sleigh with Santa Claus, and they lifted off from the roof without difficulty. As they glided towards the next house, St. Nick looked down at Jeremy and raised his eyebrows, as if to encourage the boy to ask any questions. Jeremy looked up at Santa but said nothing. All of the events that had taken place from the time that they landed on the roof until they took off happened so fast that Jeremy was struggling just to make sense of it all. At the next house, Santa Claus had Jeremy place brightly wrapped presents under the tree. There were three sleeping children in the house and they visited each one of them. St. Nicholas and his helper went from house to house. They left gifts, ate cookies, and were somehow drawn into the heads of sleeping children. Each time they were in the heads of children, Santa transformed into the conductor wearing the tuxedo and then turned back into St. Nicholas upon their exit.

Later that night as Jeremy was standing beside the conductor, Jeremy noticed that he also was wearing a crisply tailored black tuxedo with long tails. Something vibrated in the breast pocket of Jeremy's tuxedo and he cautiously put his hand into the pocket. Out of his pocket Jeremy drew a black wooden baton. Jeremy thought it looked like a magic wand that a magician or wizard would use. Without saying a word, the conductor looked down at Jeremy and gave him an encouraging nod.

Jeremy held his baton with just his thumb and index finger, just like the conductor. As Jeremy closely watched the conductor move his arms, he tried to copy the movements. The baton vibrated, communicating cues to Jeremy as to the correct movements he should make. When Jeremy did not move his baton exactly as he was supposed to, the conductor firmly tapped his baton on the podium to get Jeremy's attention. The conductor would repeat the movement again and again until Jeremy was able to replicate the maneuver to his satisfaction.

As the night went on, the stone and solemn face of the conductor had a barely detectable smile on it. Looking up at his teacher, Jeremy saw the conductor nod his head approvingly and then return his attention to the scene in front of them. While the conductor stood by his side, Jeremy focused his efforts on creating a garden. Jeremy furrowed his brow as he stared intently at the ground. After concentrating very hard, small green plants sprouted from the ground. Big red tomatoes popped out of the soil as Jeremy continued to focus his thoughts and wave his baton. Instead of ears of corn, the corn stalks sprouted tomatoes the size of softballs. Where Jeremy expected to see big orange pumpkins, he saw unnaturally large tomatoes grow before his eyes. He shook his baton with a frustrated frown on his face and tried to change the tomatoes to pumpkins.

After an icy spasm ripped through his abdomen, Jeremy knew that when he looked again at the conductor, the tuxedo would be worn by Mr. Daymo. While still holding a lit cigarette between his lips, Maestro Daymo waved the conductor's baton and said, "I was wrong: that Dr. Freud is an okay guy. The elixir he gave you has knocked down a lot of your defense mechanisms."

"Elixir?" Jeremy said.

"It's a way to turn base metals into gold. In any case, that quack's concoction has made this whole process run a lot smoother and faster. Keep taking that stuff, kid: it's liquid gold to us, so to speak!"

When Jeremy awoke, he felt as though his head was going to explode. He thought about a clown at a circus he'd seen inflating balloons from a big elongated tank of compressed air. The clown didn't take a balloon off the tank fast enough, and the balloon got larger and larger until it exploded with a loud *pop*. Feeling as though his head was being filled with air, he wondered at what point a person's head would explode like an overinflated balloon. He held his head in his hands as he shuffled towards the bathroom. When he looked in the mirror, he was shocked at what he saw. His head was of normal size. Jeremy thought for sure his head would look two or three times bigger than usual. He knew the aspirin was kept in a small glass bottle but he'd been told by his parents never to open the medicine cabinet without their permission. Jeremy and his throbbing head moved slowly to his parents' bedroom.

"Mom? Dad?" Jeremy said softly. It felt like he was shouting the words into a microphone and there were powerful speakers inside his head amplifying his voice.

His mom and dad both awoke with a start. "Jeremy! I didn't hear you. Are you okay?" his mother asked.

"Got a headache. A bad one. Can I have an aspirin?"

"Sure you can," his mother said, getting out of bed. "Did you sleep through the night? I didn't hear you last night." She looked at her husband and he shook his head: he hadn't got up during the night either.

"Yeah, I guess," Jeremy replied. Even though his mom was speaking softly, every word she said felt like a nail being pounded into his head. Jeremy was rubbing his forehead with his hands, so he didn't see the hopeful smile his mother flashed at his father.

Jeremy went to school even though the aspirin did little to relieve his headache. For the entire morning, he did his best to endure the headache. Later that morning, he looked in the bathroom mirror, still convinced his head would be at least twice its normal size. It still looked normal. In addition to the headache, he had difficulty concentrating and focusing his attention on his studies. He felt somehow disconnected. It was as if his body was running on its own and he was merely a passenger. After lunch, he was able to focus his attention better but the brunt of the throbbing headache remained.

That night Jeremy's dream was disjointed and confusing. It began as a dream about the ceiling of their house falling but transitioned into Jeremy being an ice cream cone. Mr. Daymo made a brief appearance as a talking spoon but the spoon broke into pieces and was blown away by a hearty wind. In the days that followed, Jeremy was plagued with intense headaches during the day and bizarre dreams at night.

In one dream, Jeremy was standing in the dark, shaking with fear because he knew that something or someone was chasing him. He ran, but he couldn't see where he was going. He glanced over his shoulder to see whatever was chasing him, but all he saw was darkness. He ran as fast as he could, scared of something he couldn't see or hear. Something softly wrapped around his ankle and Jeremy kicked violently at it. He never saw what it was.

Another dream found Jeremy dancing on top of a huge birthday cake to music that gradually sped up. Despite his desire to stop, he kept dancing frantically as the music's tempo increased. By the end of the of the dream, he was not so much dancing as he was having a seizure, his limbs moving wildly and no longer in time with the music.

By the following Saturday night, it seemed that as soon as Jeremy fell asleep, he immediately started dreaming. He was standing in the hospital room where he had spent a traumatic week in November. Jeremy was sitting on the side of the bed that at one time had threatened to plunge him into a black abyss. The other bed in the room was empty and Jeremy had the peculiar sensation that the entire facility had been abandoned. He didn't hear any noises or voices coming from outside of the room. There were no machines or monitors making noise.

The white linoleum floor was pristine, without a hint of dust. Jeremy noticed he was wearing a finely tailored black business suit, white dress shirt, and a black necktie. The wide black necktie was tucked into a form-fitting vest and the ensemble was topped off with an expertly tailored suit jacket made from the same dark fabric. His initial thought was, "When did Mom buy me this? I don't own a businessman's suit."

"It comes with the job," a familiar voice said from the other side of the room. Jeremy's muscles tensed, expecting a razor of pain to cut through his belly. But there was no pain this time when Mr. Daymo appeared. His muscles gradually relaxed and Jeremy looked in the direction of the voice. One corner of the room was darker than the rest of the white room. It was as if all of the light that brightly bathed the hospital room was somehow incapable of extending into the portion of the room where Mr. Daymo stood. In the soft light of the lit cigarette that he held in his mouth, Jeremy saw that Mr. Daymo was once again wearing the finely tailored suit Jeremy first saw when the two met in his hospital room the previous November.

"You're finally ready," Mr. Daymo said, flicking a bit of ash from his cigarette, which landed in the well-lit portion of the room. "I guess you could call this your graduation day. Today is when you say good-bye to your alma mater."

"Alma what?"

"Alma mater: it's a kind of song." Mr. Daymo took a long draw from his cigarette and then exhaled. The scent of burned cantaloupe filled the hospital room. "And speaking of songs, you're now ready to be a conductor of sorts. A stage manager. The world's greatest party organizer. I guess you could say that you'll be the host with the most, young man!"

"But I…I…" Jeremy stuttered.

The man held out his hand as if to say *stop*. "I know what

you're going to say. You're not sure what you're doing. You feel ill-prepared for the task at hand. All those feelings are very natural, believe me. We've all felt that way when we first got started. Just let it happen and don't fight it."

Jeremy's heart leapt into his mouth and he was frightened. "Am I...dying? Are you telling me to just let myself die?"

Mr. Daymo laughed uproariously and slapped his thigh with his open hand. "You're so funny! You're a stitch! No, Jeremy, you are very much a living creature! You see, the Secret Club is much larger than just you and me. You are now one of us. And I can assure you, we are all very much alive!"

"What am I supposed to do?" Jeremy asked.

"It'll become clear to you. I guess you might say that you'll be a Michelangelo to the blank canvas that is the mind. You'll create canvases that run the gamut from the sweet to the horrendous."

"What's a gamut?"

"It's a series of musical notes: C major to G minor."

"I...I..." Jeremy stammered.

"Remember this fact: if the members of the Secret Club stopped doing our jobs, people on this planet would never be the same. Capeesh?"

"Does capeesh mean *do you understand*?"

"That's my boy!" Mr. Daymo said, slapping his thigh. He turned his back on Jeremy and appeared to walk right through the wall and out of the room. As he disappeared, Jeremy heard Mr. Daymo's metal lighter flick open and then shut.

After Mr. Daymo walked through the wall of the hospital room that night, Jeremy never had another dream of his own.

The lights in the hospital room intensified. Soon, Jeremy was engulfed in a blinding white light. He felt as though he was swimming in an endless ocean of white light. Even holding up his hand to shade his eyes did not provide any relief, and Jeremy couldn't see anything but white glare for quite some time.

When the light finally subsided, Jeremy found himself standing in an empty white room. There was no furniture, no doors, no windows, and no indication as to the purpose of the room. In fact, he wasn't sure if he was even in a *room* in the first place. Spinning around a few times, Jeremy couldn't detect where the ceiling met the walls. There likewise was nowhere he could see where the walls met the floor. Was there any floor at all? What was he standing on? He spun around again but saw nothing. During his third scan around the room, Jeremy saw a little boy. The child didn't look quite old enough to be in kindergarten. The toddler was wearing baby blue flannel pajamas that had the feet sewn into them.

"Hey," Jeremy called out to the boy, "where are we?"

After a lengthy silence, the child said something, but it didn't seem to be in response to Jeremy's question. "I'm so tired. So tired," the little boy lamented. Although he was looking directly at Jeremy, the toddler gave no indication that he saw him. The little boy stood there, looking forward with a blank expression on his face. Jeremy walked over to the child and waved his hand in front of the kid's face but there was still no indication he could see him. Jeremy lightly pushed the boy's shoulder and the child awkwardly fell backwards, landing firmly on his rump. The little boy looked surprised and scrunched up his face as if he was going to cry but he didn't.

"Stop it," the toddler said to no one in particular, slapping at the air with his hands.

Gently, Jeremy helped lift the boy to his feet and the child just stood there in the white room, once again looking blankly ahead and showing no emotion. For a few moments, Jeremy and the little boy just stood in the white room in silence. Jeremy kept waiting for something to happen, but nothing did.

Jeremy felt something vibrate in his right hand and when he

looked down, a conductor's baton was vibrating in his hand. It felt like the baton was a little bird that was trying to escape Jeremy's hand so it could fly away. The baton fluttered against Jeremy's grip. Instead of holding the baton tighter, Jeremy decided to loosen his grip a little on the baton. Feeling a sense of inspiration, Jeremy began to wave the baton through the air. He began to draw large-as-life pictures, using the baton was a large paintbrush. He drew a black and white outline of a tree and stepped back from it, amazed at how realistic it looked.

Jeremy heard the little boy's voice. He turned to the child, who was still standing in the same place. Even though he could see that the toddler wasn't moving his lips, in Jeremy's head, he heard the little boy's voice.

"Toys. Green. Lots of green stuff. The grass feels hard and crispy. Sun is warm. Oatmeal is good. Beets. Blech."

As the stream of spoken thoughts continued, it became faster and faster, until it sounded like the high pitched whine of mosquitoes flying around Jeremy's ears. Jeremy felt a surge of energy in his body as the trilling falsetto sound intensified. Jeremy and the baton glided around the white room, spreading wide swaths of color. The two were working in unison: Jeremy guided the baton and the baton guided Jeremy. As the soundtrack of the child's thoughts raced through Jeremy's head, things began to take shape in the room.

In just a few seconds, the pristine white room was a detailed and colorful landscape. It looked for the most part like a campsite next to a lake except there were things that looked out of place. At the edge of the lake stood a yellow refrigerator whose motor was so loud that Jeremy thought it was surely on its last leg. A sea serpent stuck its head out of the water and Jeremy knew intuitively this was the Loch Ness Monster. The little boy was no longer in his trance and he was pointing at the monster as he giggled. The huge scaly serpent delighted the child instead of frightening him. It was bright pink with yellow stripes and was wearing a sea serpent-sized sombrero.

With the high pitched whine of unseen insects reverberating in his ears, Jeremy created additional details to the campsite including a talking teddy bear holding a fishing rod, a tree that sprouted Rice Krispie bars instead of leaves and two adults dancing a polka around a campfire. When the monster dove under the water, the little boy ran to the old refrigerator. He pulled clumsily on the door but it didn't open.

"No food until supper!" the pair of polka dancing adults sang in unison.

The Loch Ness Monster stuck its head out of the lake and barked like a dog before dipping back into the water. While lying in the sand next to the water with his fishing pole, the teddy bear said, "Candy. Candy." Jeremy watched as the child interacted with the things and characters in the scene. An even higher-pitched whine insulted Jeremy's ears. He began to wildly move his other hand around, quickly erasing the lake scene and replacing it with a small bedroom.

The little boy sat on a bed that was at least ten times bigger than a normal sized bed. When the child eased himself off the side of the bed, he had a drop of about five feet to the carpeted floor. As if in a trance, the little boy slowly approached a closet door at the other end of the room.

When Jeremy waved his baton, twangy country and western music started playing. As the boy reached the closet door, he held out a trembling hand and prepared to open it. Before he could do so, the closet door burst open, slamming against the wall with a loud *bang*. Behind the door was a dark tunnel that appeared to be very very long. Cool and moldy smelling air came out of the tunnel and the little boy tried to retreat. His feet were glued to the floor, however, so he could do nothing but gaze into the terrifying abyss.

When he saw movement and something emerging from the darkness, the little boy whimpered in fear. Before he could see what was emerging out of the tunnel's darkness, everything turned to black. Jeremy and the little boy were floating in the darkness and as the little boy yawned, he said, "Me so tired." So he closed his eyes and went to sleep.

CHAPTER FIFTEEN

The Search for Jeremy

Mr. and Mrs. Bracken slept through the night and they awoke refreshed. Mrs. Bracken went to Jeremy's room, yawning and stretching her arms.

"Jeremy? Time to get up, hon."

Jeremy wasn't in his bedroom. One of his blankets had slid off of the bed and was laying on the floor. Mrs. Bracken picked it up, folded it, and laid it on his bed. There was nothing she saw in her son's bedroom that caused Mrs. Bracken any concern. She walked into the kitchen, and when Jeremy wasn't at the table with a bowl of cereal, she called out to him a little louder. "Jeremy? Where are you?"

Mr. Bracken shuffled into the kitchen and started making coffee. "Did you check the sofa downstairs?" he asked his wife.

When her son wasn't asleep on the downstairs couch, panic hit her. His parents frantically searched the small house, looking in the closets and even under Jeremy's bed. Still wearing their pajamas, Mr. and Mrs. Bracken went outside, looking around the house and the adjacent yards. While Mr. Bracken continued to search outside, Mrs. Bracken ran back into the house and started making phone calls. Ten minutes later, two squad cars were at their house and three uniformed police officers had joined the search. They found nothing was missing from the house other than Jeremy. As far as Mrs. Bracken could tell, all of his clothes were either in the hamper or in his chest-of-drawers. He owned two pairs of shoes and both pair were still in his closet. His most prized possession, an autographed football, was sitting undisturbed on top of his dresser.

Very early in the process of trying to locate the boy, the police started referring to this as a case of a runaway child. By the end of that first day, most of the authorities began routinely using the phrase "*the runaway Bracken boy*" when referring to the case.

All of the standard efforts were made by the authorities and the community to find the boy who had run away from home. A photograph of Jeremy taken by his father the previous Christmas was shown on all three television stations during their local news programs. A copy of that snapshot, which showed Jeremy happily holding a new G.I. Joe, was taped to the dashboard of every one of the city's squad cars. A pond about a mile from his home was dredged. Despite these efforts, no trace of Jeremy was ever found.

The police detective assigned to the case was experienced and very thorough. He spoke to the child's parents, friends, teacher, and other relatives, trying to find the clue that would lead him to the boy. Mrs. Bracken told the detective about her son's recent medical treatment and gave him Dr. Freud's business card. He made a long distance phone call to the university where Dr. Ford Freud worked, hoping that his expertise in pediatric psychology might be able to uncover a clue that had been missed.

After the detective provided a summary of the investigation, Dr. Freud sighed in disappointment. "Unfortunately, my analysis of the situation will not provide much hope to you or to the parents of the patient," Dr. Freud lamented. "There was an underlying personality disorder in this patient, which would fall under the general classification of an anti-social disorder. If I were to define this in layman's terms that you would understand, this is where the patient exhibits non-conformist behavior that is self-centered and only to his benefit. In Master Bracken's case, I discovered a deeply held anti-social tendency, which manifested itself in attention-seeking behavior and ultimately to the theft of his father's pistol. I concluded that his histrionic stories about nightmares and his overall pathologic behavior were triggered by problems with post-operative pain from a bowel resection."

"How were you able to prove that the surgery caused the child's change in behavior?" the detective asked.

"Through the application of long-held scientific principles. There is obviously no medical test to conclusively prove this, of course. For example, I know for a fact that there are no monsters who hide under the beds of children, but I do not have a scientific test to establish this well-known fact."

"I understand."

"Detective, is the gun that was used by the patient missing from the home?"

"No. Mr. Bracken showed us the weapon and advised us that ever since the incident, he kept it either on his person or in the trunk of his car at all times," the detective replied.

"That fact further supports my conclusions. By appropriately taking away the gun, the patient's anti-social outlet was successfully thwarted, thus the patient had to find another source for his pathologic personality disorder to express itself. Without access to the gun, this patient required another type of malignant manifestation. This situation was likely made even more volatile because his parents hopefully were requiring the patient to take the medication that I had prescribed for him."

"Yes, they mentioned to me that he had been taking a new medication for more than a week," the detective said.

"Precisely. The medication was working as it should, causing disassociation of the patient's thought processes and thereby challenging the underlying personality disorder. Since he could not avoid taking the therapeutic medication that I prescribed while he was under the control of his parents, he had to find a way to escape the therapeutic effects of the treatment. By running away from home, his anti-social personality disorder would be unfettered and allowed to thrive. Although I am deeply saddened by this patient's actions, it is not completely unforeseeable."

The detective paused and carefully chose the words for his next question. "Dr. Freud, did you warn the Brackens that this was a foreseeable possibility?" When there was no immediate response from the doctor, the detective added, "Did they know that this might happen?"

There was another uncomfortable pause in the conversation and then Dr. Freud said, "Well…neither an experienced practitioner nor even a parent can anticipate every action that may be taken by a child who has a personality disorder. If you have children, sir, you know they are an unpredictable lot. There is simply no way science can predict that a patient in the future will conduct himself in a certain way."

The detective thanked the doctor for his time and concluded the interview. It was a surprise to the detective when he received a bill from Dr. Freud for their thirty minute telephone conversation. Instead of throwing it away, the detective put the bill in the official case file.

Six weeks was the standard period of time for a missing persons case to be kept open. During that time, all of the likely places for a runaway child to turn up were checked multiple times including bus stations, YMCAs, jails, the youth authority, and the city morgue. By the time the case file was closed as *unresolved*, it wasn't just a cold case: it was ice cold. Despite their best efforts, there was absolutely no lead that shed any light on the disappearance. Busybodies in the neighborhood told macabre tales of children being lured into opium dens by hippies. Most of those who were involved in the case in an official capacity predicted that Jeremy would wash up in a lake or river within a year or so. No body was ever found.

For months, Jeremy's mother was sure her son was going to walk into the house at any moment. Every sound she heard at night heralded that Jeremy had finally come home. She insisted on keeping both the front and back doors to the house unlocked, even at night. She began sleeping on the couch so that the front door was the last thing that she saw before falling asleep and the first thing she saw when she awoke. Even after taking these measures, she slept very little. Every night consisted of short periods of sleep, which were interrupted each time she heard a sound from outside or a creak in the house. Although she couldn't remember all of the dreams she had during that stressful time, there were two that were especially vivid. She experienced these two dreams multiple times and they were always in black and white.

In one dream, she was sitting on the couch when Jeremy waltzed through the front door as if nothing had happened. "Hi, mom!" he said happily.

"Where have you been?" she asked her son, launching herself off the couch and hugging him.

"What do you mean? I never left. I've been sleeping downstairs the past month. You must have just missed seeing me."

While she was dreaming, this explanation seemed entirely plausible. He had been there all the time but she'd simply never crossed paths with her son during that time. When she woke up, the plausibility of this story quickly evaporated. Even so, she would always check his bedroom and the basement.

In the other dream, Jeremy came home and he was now a young man. He looked like he was fifteen or sixteen years old.

"The government drafted me to go to Vietnam."

"But the draft is over," she said.

"Yeah, now that the war is done, the government's drafting kids to teach English to the Vietnamese. I did my time, got an honorable discharge, and now I'm back home."

Once again, this story seemed very logical and plausible while she was in the midst of the dream. But once again, the waking world quickly and cruelly exposed the dream as nothing more than a mother's wishful fantasy.

Because she refused to leave the house for any reason for fear of missing Jeremy's return, her husband took over several additional household tasks such as grocery shopping just to keep the household running. Three months after Jeremy ran away, she required hospitalization for what the doctors officially labeled "extreme emotional exhaustion." The combined effects of medication, electroshock therapy, and counseling eventually reduced her anxiety and sorrow to a level wherein she was able to leave the house for short periods of time.

Although he wasn't a religious man, Jeremy's father convinced himself that Jeremy's disappearance was somehow a punishment imposed on him for something he did or failed to do for his son. He reasoned that if he worked even harder than usual, he would somehow be rewarded with the return of his son. As he reckoned a man should, Mr. Bracken was strong and did not cry in front of anyone.

He nearly had an unacceptable display of his grief the following Halloween. When a little boy dressed as Batman came to the door, he rushed to the bathroom and wept as he laid on the cold tile floor, but that was the only time that he was in danger of breaking down in front of others. He was successful in swallowing his anguish and keeping it hidden inside of himself. When this bitter pill finally bore a hole through his stomach lining, he began popping an antacid into his mouth as frequently as a chain smoker lit up a cigarette.

Six months to the day that Jeremy ran away, Mrs. Bracken was still sleeping on the couch. Every night she stared at the door, willing it to suddenly open and for her son to come through it. That night, she eventually fell asleep and as she dreamt, she tossed around on the lumpy, uncomfortable couch. This dream was different from all the others because it was colorful and bright. She was on a small sailboat that was speedily leaving an island. There was a boy standing on the island's beach, knee deep in the dark blue water. Even though he was far away, she knew instantly it was her son. Having never been on a sailboat, she had no idea how to steer it. She tried to move the rudder so that the boat would return to the island.

"Jeremy!" she screamed in both happiness and frustration.

She pulled on the boat's ropes randomly, trying in vain to turn the boat around. Although her son was becoming smaller and smaller, when she looked behind her, she somehow could clearly see his facial features. As if she was looking through binoculars, she could clearly see that he had a broad smile on his face as he waved goodbye to her. She tried to jump out of the boat and swim to him, but she couldn't move her body despite her desperate struggle to do so. Somehow she was stuck firmly to the boat that was whisking her away from her son.

Just as she began to cry in her dream, her son's voice whispered in her ears, "I'm okay. Don't worry about me. I'm okay. Honest Injun." She twisted her head around because it sounded like Jeremy was right next to her. Becky Bracken was certain that she could feel his breath on her ear as he whispered to her. But there was no one else in the boat. As the sailboat moved faster and faster, the island disappeared into the horizon. Mrs. Bracken held her arms out towards the island as it slipped out of view. The water turned pink, as if she was floating in a fruit punch.

Since she wasn't looking forward, she was startled when the boat ran aground on another island. When the boat hit land, it vaulted her onto the soft white sandy beach. The island's trees were shedding their red and tan foliage, and she smelled the wonderful scent of burning autumn leaves. Her legs felt very weak, so she crawled on the warm sand. A pack of four Labrador retrievers emerged from the tree line and barked as they ran towards her. As they launched themselves at her, Mrs. Bracken held up her hands to protect her face but the dogs managed to avoid them. She fell down on the beach, the dogs licking her face as they made excited whining noises. As they continued to happily lick her face and neck, she began to laugh. She hadn't laughed for a very long time and it sounded strange to her.

She felt like she could stand and after she did so, the dogs nuzzled her legs playfully and licked her calves. A large table appeared on the beach, which was covered with mounds of colorful fruits and vegetables, some she didn't even recognize. Mr. Bracken was sitting at the table, wearing a colorful Hawaiian shirt and holding up a glass of red wine. He smiled at her and encouraged her to join him. When she reached the table, her husband handed her a cold bottle of Coke.

"Welcome, my dear," he said, smiling widely. "I'm so glad you're here with me!"

The theme song for the television show *Happy Days* began blaring from hundreds of unseen speakers. A gleeful singer said the name of each day of the week, followed by the peppy refrain "Happy Days!" Her husband held out his wine glass and she tapped it with her bottle of Coke. When she drank the soda, she tasted nothing but she started to feel very warm all over her body, as if she had just stepped into a sauna. When she woke up on the couch, she felt clammy and she was covered in sweat.

The same night as his wife's sailing adventure, Mr. Bracken also had a dream. He rarely remembered any of his dreams, and it was for this reason he never questioned his son's claim that he couldn't remember any of his. All of his dreams were in black and white, and to his knowledge, this was true of everyone's dreams.

On this night, he had a vivid and colorful dream for the first and last time in his life. In the dream, he was at work, sitting at his metal desk. Instead of writing reports, however, he was trying to build something using Lego building blocks. There was a drawing of a large abstract shape pinned to the bulletin board and he knew that it was his job to use the Legos to build a structure that looked like that shape. He looked at his small stack of Legos and then at the picture, concluding there was no way he could make the structure with what he had.

A man wearing a denim shirt and well-worn jeans walked up to his desk. He had a tattered tan cowboy hat. David Bracken recognized the man as country and western singer Don Williams.

"Here you go," Mr. Williams said, placing a box of Legos on his desk.

Mr. Bracken ran his hands through the generous collection of Legos. "Yes, this will work," he said. "Now I can do it!"

"You sure can," Don Williams remarked. "You can do it just fine."

He looked up to thank Mr. Williams and was surprised to see the singer's face had developed some of Jeremy's facial features. The man who looked like a cross between his son and Don Williams smiled and started to sing Don Williams' biggest hit: *You're My Best Friend*. As he sang, the man turned around and started to walk away. Mr. Bracken wanted to hug the man, but when he tried to rise from his chair, he could not. For some reason he couldn't control the muscles in his body, so he just remained sitting in the chair. It was then that he noticed that he was very tired. He decided to put his head down on his desk and go to sleep. He would take a little nap and then try to catch up with the man.

Before and after Jeremy's vanishing, the Brackens didn't talk about the dreams or nightmares they experienced. Mr. Bracken could rarely remember his dreams, and Mrs. Bracken was embarrassed to talk about hers. As a result, they never told each other about the dreams they had on the six month anniversary of Jeremy's disappearance.

The announcement of Becky Bracken's pregnancy eleven months after Jeremy ran away from home was quite a surprise to everyone. Dr. Glover told them years ago that it was unlikely she would get pregnant after Jeremy's birth. The Brackens decided they couldn't bear to raise a child in what they felt was "Jeremy's House." There were only two bedrooms in the house and the thought of setting up a nursery in Jeremy's room was too painful to consider.

They left a sealed envelope with the elderly couple who purchased the house. The new owners promised to give the envelope to Jeremy if he should come back home. In the envelope was a letter from his parents begging Jeremy to contact them. Their new address and phone number were printed in dark black letters along with a twenty dollar bill, in case he needed money to get back to them.

The new owners kept the envelope in the cabinet above the refrigerator where Mrs. Bracken stored Jeremy's Halloween candy. When the house was sold six years later, the buyers thoroughly cleaned the house before taking possession. The envelope with Jeremy's name printed on it was thrown away. Unopened.

AFTERWORD TO BOOK ONE

By Dr. Ford Freud, PhD., M.D., C.P.A., B.M.F., S.N.O.T. (President)

You hold in your hands a slanderous collection of lies. I have just read the preview version of Mr. Ford's book and I am outraged! After finishing it, I immediately called the publisher and did my best to stop its printing. I was told there was nothing that I could do except pen an afterward that they graciously agreed to insert into the back of this terrible tome. There are so many outlandish accusations and half-truths included in this book, I do not know where to begin! You have no idea how much self control it is taking for me not to hunt Mr. Ford down and physically assault his person in a most rough and violent manner!

This scandalous author has the audacity to suggest that my scientific approach to this patient was flawed. He thereupon goes into a fantastical and fictional depiction of this patient's thought processes, clinical course, and eventual outcome. This book should have been based on science and fact, *not* folly and speculation!

Those of you who know me and know of the important work I have conducted in the field will recognize this publication for what it is: a tawdry piece of fiction served to the public as if it was entirely factual. Those of you who have had the opportunity to be taught by me will instantly realize that the physician described by Mr. Ford is a mockery of my true self. I am particularly concerned that this parody of me will be accepted as truth by readers who are unenlightened with my body of work. For those of you who fit into that category, I ask humbly that you not rely upon this trash publication as a true representation of my demeanor or skills. Instead, you should go in haste to your closest university library and see what my learned contemporaries have written about me and my work. I suggest that you read any or all of the following in order to cleanse your palate:

The Human Brain: Swiss Cheese or Cottage Cheese? The Physician's Guide to Dark Thoughts, Stain-producing Emotions, Bizarre Ideations and the Unreliable Memory, by Dr. B. A. Paradis.

Did You Just Lock the Door Behind Me? The Personal Diary of an Unjustly Incarcerated Insane Asylum Patient, by Dr. C. A. Grimes.

A Confounded Mind in a Confounded World: A Student's Guide to Preeminently Educated Psychologists and Acutely Clever Mental Health Professionals, edited by Dr. Germana Aurora.

I have recently had my student research assistants conduct a background check on the author selected by this publisher and what they discovered is horrifying. Since Mr. Ford has deemed it appropriate to slander my good name, I feel compelled to respond in kind. First and foremost, he is a licensed attorney, as opposed to a psychologist or a physician. Though he has earned a *Juris Doctorate* degree, everyone knows that this not truly a doctorate level program. Ask Mr. Ford to show you a copy of his doctoral dissertation. He won't be able to because JDs do not write dissertations. It is widely accepted that without authoring a doctoral dissertation, you simply cannot be considered a doctor of *anything*. Parents, this is what happens to the minds of your children if they are permitted to be taught by Jesuits in a law school! Additionally, I have learned that he is from the Midwest, an area of our country that is backwards and unenlightened. He likely would not know the difference between Titian (the painter) and Titan (the moon of Jupiter)!

My final entreaty to you is that you burn this book. Through the ages, small minded and short-sighted people have wrongly burned books. The book that you now hold in your hands, however, deserves to be torched, as this is the only way to be assured that no one might be lured into reading this travesty. However, I believe you should destroy it with your personal safety in mind. I therefore recommend that you safely destroy it in your fireplace or local shaman's sacrificial burning pit that you can find in your area.

In addition, it is your duty as a forward-thinking and erudite member of this society to make sure no other unsuspecting soul is affronted by this blasphemous tome. Therefore, I entreat you to seek out and purchase every copy of this book that you can locate, whether it be located at a reputable bookseller, a less than reputable bookseller, garage sale or thrift store. It is your solemn duty to our society to purchase and destroy every copy of this book you can find, lest the world be sullied by the lies contained therein.

Friends, make sure that no one is subjected to this book of lies. Your duty, fair reader, is to burn this book, bury the ashes, and cover the ashes with salt so that naught may ever grow in that ground.

I am yours respectfully,
yet mortified,
Dr. Ford Freud

ABOUT THE AUTHORS

Dr. Ford Freud, MD, PHD, DC, etc.

Dr. Freud is a world-renowned psychiatrist, physician, professor, and competitive dog groomer. He has earned degrees and awards too numerous to list in this little box. He understands and treats all forms of psychopathology, including phobias, anxiety, personality disorders, and the pernicious desire to collect postage stamps. You wish you were as smart as Dr. Ford Freud. But you're not.

J. A. FORD

Mr. Ford went to school for a long time and managed to obtain a number of meaningless degrees and certificates of participation. Mr. Ford wears shoes when he is writing books. They are always shoes that have laces because he has an irrational fear of loafers, especially those with little tassels on them. He sleeps wearing a homemade tinfoil skullcap so that he is protected from twisted dreams and disturbing nightmares.

ACKNOWLEDGMENTS

You might be surprised to learn that writing a book is not entirely a solitary endeavor. A number of people worked with me or otherwise influenced the creation of this book and I am indebted to each of them.

My Beta readers: Craig Grimes, Bryant Paradis, and Dawn Ford. In addition to my wife, these people read the various drafts of the book and used their talents to polish the story. Craig spent hours with me drinking Coke Zero and dealing with story structure. Without a doubt, this book is better due to their efforts.

Authors in Kansas City: KB Draper, Brian Peterson, and Ted Nowak. As I was getting started, these local authors were very gracious with their time. They provided advice, encouragement, and a huge amount of information about writing and publishing. Also, author Quincy Allen provided helpful guidance. The books of all of these talented authors are available on Amazon and I recommend that you check them out.

My social media maven: Paul Wegener.

My partners at Mascot Books: Naren Aryal, Maria Waksmunski, and Daniel Wheatley.

Finally, the authors who sparked my desire to write and who shaped my storytelling technique: Edgar Allan Poe, Stephen King, and Lemony Snicket.